KT-460-299

Berlitz®

Amsterdam

Front cover: Keizersgracht canal

Right: Traditional canalside architecture

TOP 10 ATTRACTIONS

Anne Frank House • Visit the house in which she wrote her extraordinary diary *(page 66)*

The Dam • This square is the symbolic heart of the city and home to the ornate Koninklijk Paleis *(page 62)*

Oude Kerk • Dating from the early 13th century it is the oldest church in the city *(page 29)*

Begijnhof • Find peace and quiet in the picturesque courtyard, notable for its quaint architecture *(page 60)*

A canal cruise · A leisurely way to see the sights *(page 117)*

Van Gogh Museum · Houses a collection of hundreds of the troubled artist's works *(page 56)*

Bloemenmarkt · Colourful flowers on display all year round *(page 50)*

Hortus Botanicus · This botanical garden in the Plantage district houses more than 4,000 species of plants *(page 44)*

Rijksmuseum · Though under restoration, this is still the place to see the finest Dutch masterpieces *(page 53)*

NEMO Science Centre · Get your hands on the latest science and technology in this remarkable ship-shaped museum *(page 48)*

CONTENTS

38

53

42

INTRODUCTION

There's no other city on earth like Amsterdam. It is a city of superlatives, having more canals than Venice and more bridges than Paris. It is also one of the prettiest cities in Europe. More than 50 museums – featuring everything from the world's most prominent artists to the history of cannabis – quench the thirst of even the most ardent culture buff, and with 7,000 buildings from the 16th, 17th and 18th centuries, the reflections of its illustrious past happily ripple on into the 21st century. However, the lure of Amsterdam's bricks and mortar is only part of its excitement. Its contemporary culture is vibrant – it's definitely not a city stuck in the past, and its people are open-minded, easygoing and strong-minded but also down to earth and welcoming to visitors.

Amsterdam was founded where the outlet of the River Amstel met the salty tidal waters of the Zuiderzee. With little dry land to build on, exactly why a small group of settlers chose this unpromising spot is difficult to understand. Yet it proved to be an excellent decision, since Amsterdammers very soon came to control the waters of the river and the trade

> ### Waterworld
>
> Amsterdam contains more than 1,200 bridges crossing more than 100 canals, which have a combined length of over 100km (65 miles).

that flowed along it. By the 17th century, Amsterdam had become arguably the richest city in the world, at the centre of a far-flung Dutch colonial empire. It traded in spices, rum and sugar cane among other commodities, and its residents demanded only the best. The Amsterdam of this period – the Golden Age – forms the heart of today's city.

Amsterdam is home to more than half a million bicycles

Soaring townhouses

Without doubt, a major attraction of the city is its historic buildings. The lines of tall, narrow houses with their pretty gables rest beside picture-perfect tree-lined canals. They are connected by humpback bridges and quaint cobbled walkways, which seem to have changed little in nearly 400 years – in fact, since they were walked by such inhabitants as the artist Rembrandt and the explorer Abel Tasman, who gave his name to Tasmania.

Amsterdam is a wonderful city for visitors. It's small enough to stroll around, and, with the canalside streets too narrow for tour buses, there's no risk of sightseers driving past all the best attractions at high speed. You have to feel the summer sun or see your breath on a crisp winter morning as you step out to see what Amsterdam is all about. If you take a canal tour, the quiet boats allow you to admire the architecture from water-level, floating slowly along away from the noise of the modern world.

The museums could keep you busy for weeks. Art collections, historic houses and memorials to heroes and heroines can all be found here. For entertainment after the sun sets, there are more than 40 different performances in the city every evening. The Netherlands Opera and the National Ballet are based here, and there are numerous orchestral, musical and comedy venues, along with revues and dance shows. Amsterdam also plays host to one of the most dynamic club scenes in Europe.

A Living City

The façades of the buildings may hark back to the past, but the interiors do not. Internet banking, interactive information points and recycling advice centres – the concepts of today are alive and thriving all around the city. This is no historic ghost town: the city brims with people. Its houses are still lived in (although most are now apartments rather than single-family homes), and its streets filled with bakeries, delicatessens and wine merchants where people drop in to buy dinner on the way home in the evening. It's all part of the fascinating dichotomy you find at every turn here. The city strides into the future while still holding metaphorical hands with the past.

The historic heart of Amsterdam has remained relatively unchanged mainly because of people power. In the latter part of the 20th century, as in most cities, property developers were coveting interesting locations and in Amsterdam they

Barges on the Oosterdok

had their eyes on the old canal houses, knowing they could make a tidy profit by demolishing them and replacing them with something modern. Unfashionable buildings, such as the warehouses of the old docks, were left to the elements. Some Amsterdammers, though, had other ideas. They took to the streets to fight for their city, barricading historic houses and occupying empty buildings in the warehouse district.

This was typical of the populace, and it wasn't the first time; Amsterdammers have been standing up for what they believe in for centuries. When Protestants were persecuted in the 16th century, they flocked here from all over Europe to take refuge. During World War II, the dock workers of Amsterdam went on strike as an act of protest against the Nazis' treatment of the Jews in the city. Although in the end the protest was futile, it shows the strength of feeling and social awareness that pervades every part of society here.

Illuminated bridge across the Singel canal

Today, Amsterdam has over 100 different nationalities living within the city boundaries, a situation that could be fraught with difficulty and strain. Yet here it has added to the cultural richness built up over centuries of exploration and trade. That doesn't mean to say the city is free from racism, tensions between ethnic groups and concerns about immigration; all of these are perceived to have increased since the murder of filmmaker Theo van Gogh by an Islamic fundamentalist in 2004.

Amsterdammers seem to have the ability to find creative solutions to their problems. When there wasn't enough housing on the land, they looked at the empty canals and decided that houseboats would help. There are now more than 2,500 on the city's waterways. When cars became a problem in the old town they gave the bicycle priority, and now there are more than 500,000 cycles on the streets – and an estimated 30,000 at the bottom of the canal system at any one time.

Amsterdammers fight for everyone's rights against oppression, or the right of David to stand against the faceless Goliath of bureaucracy. In fact in Amsterdam when several thousand Davids get together to form a pressure group, Goliath has to sit up and take notice. Amsterdam is a city of 21st-century pressures, such as the problems of traffic and litter – but the problems are faced realistically, debated by the community, and agreed solutions are put into action. When the solutions

Holland or the Netherlands?

Are you in the Netherlands or are you in Holland – or are the two terms interchangeable? No. To a Dutchman the word Holland doesn't mean the whole country: that's the Netherlands. The country is divided into 12 provinces, of which North Holland and South Holland are two. Amsterdam is in North Holland, hence all the tourist literature that features the word 'Holland' and contributes to the confusion.

In the Papeneiland Café

don't work, the process starts again. It is all seen as a huge learning curve.

Of course, the residents of Amsterdam don't spend all their time waving protest banners. Many are as industrious and hardworking as their forefathers. They enjoy galleries and exhibitions as much as the visitors do – it can be hard to get tickets for performances because of local demand. And they love to socialise. Bars – particularly the 'brown bars' – are popular places in which to meet and put the world to rights. In summer, everyone drinks outside at tables in the squares and on the streets. Sit down and you'll soon be engaged in conversation (most Amsterdammers speak good English).

Amsterdam has many facets. Yet these seem to amalgamate into a coherent whole. It is a city of history, which shouts from every gable and street corner; a city of culture – of museums and musicians and artists; a city of learning with a large university; a city of trade with banking at its core; a multi-ethnic city of over 100 different nationalities; a generally tolerant city, in which minority groups have a chance to flourish; and a city of tourism, with more than 10 million foreign visitors per year. The beauty of its buildings is undisputed, but it is the sum of all these parts that makes Amsterdam an unforgettable place to visit.

A BRIEF HISTORY

It is difficult to think of a less promising spot for what has become one of the world's major cities. Something must have been appealing about the marshy outlet of the River Amstel where it met the IJ (pronounced 'Aye'), a tidal inlet of the Zuiderzee – even although the area flooded on a regular basis with water forced in by the prevailing winter winds.

The Batavians, a Germanic tribe, travelled down the Rhine to found the first settlements in the river delta around 50BC. The land was entered on maps of the Roman Empire but, following Rome's decline, became the domain of various Germanic tribes in the Dark Ages. This probably had little effect on the settlements, whose main trade was fishing.

From Fishing to Trading

By around AD1000, the land we now call the Netherlands was ruled by a number of feudal lords, who had total power over the land and the people who lived on it. The first wooden houses were built on the site of Amsterdam in around AD1200, on artificial mounds called *terps*. The town was fortified against rival lords and against the seawater, the River Amstel being dammed at what is now the square called the Dam. This was not just to control the tides but also to manipulate trade, as it prevented seagoing ships from taking their goods up the river – they had to transfer the goods to locally owned boats for their journey. It gave the local populace a healthy income and began two important elements in the city's history: the predominance of the merchant classes and the use of barges for inland trade.

In 1275 the settlement of Amstelredamme (one of the names by which it was known) received permission from Count Floris V of Holland to transport goods on the River

Amstel without incurring tolls, giving the city a monopoly on trade along the river. In 1323 Amstelredamme became a toll-free port for beer and, once a method of preserving herring had been perfected in the late 14th century, the town also had a product with a high profit margin and began exporting fish around Europe.

The early 15th century saw a healthy expansion of trade, and the population rose dramatically. Catastrophic fires destroyed a large part of the city in 1421 and again in 1452. Following the second fire, legislation made it illegal to build with wood, and brick became the material of choice. Today only a few wooden buildings remain from before the 15th-century fires. Het Houten Huys in the Begijnhof is considered to be the oldest. The legislation brought about a feast of civil engineering projects, including the building of the city wall, incorporating the Waag and Schreierstoren in *c*.1480.

The Oude Kerk, Amsterdam's oldest church

The Arrival of the Spanish

Meanwhile the political climate was changing with a series of dynastic intermarriages. Philip of Burgundy began to bring some semblance of unification to the Low Countries (the region that roughly translates to the Netherlands and Belgium) in the 1420s. He was succeeded by Charles the Bold, whose daughter Maria married into the House of Habsburg. Her son Philip married Isabella of Spain and in 1500 she gave birth to Charles, the future Charles V, ruler of the Netherlands, Holy Roman Emperor, but more importantly, Charles I, King of Spain and all her dominions – an empire on which it was said the sun never set.

Spanish rule was ruthless but, for a while, Amsterdam was left alone. Its position as an important trading post kept it apart from the more barbarous behaviour in other areas. It saw a threefold increase in its population as refugees flooded in from other parts of the empire. Diamond polishers from Antwerp and Jews from Portugal brought their influences to the city.

Amsterdam was already developing a reputation of tolerance, as these new and disparate groups settled into the city. At the same time, Martin Luther's new Christian doctrine, Protestantism, was spreading like wildfire across Europe. The teachings of the French Protestant theologian John Calvin took a firm hold in the northern provinces of the Low Countries. It was at this time that Huguenots (French Protestants) came to Amsterdam, fleeing from persecution in their own country.

The Catholic Spanish cracked down on the heretical followers of Calvin, and in 1535 there were anti-papacy demonstrations on the Dam. Strict Catholic leaders took control of the city, and in 1567 Charles V's successor, Philip II, initiated an anti-heresy campaign: Calvinism was outlawed, and repression was ruthless.

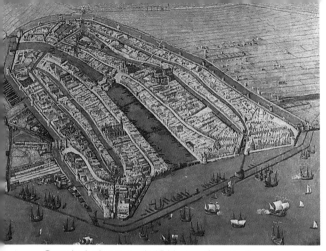

Cornelis Anthoniszoon's 1544 map of Amsterdam

Towards Independence

This atmosphere of intense fear and violence sowed the seeds of revolt. The House of Orange (with a power base around the small town in the south of France) had claim to lands in the Low Countries, and one member, William the Silent, began to organise opposition to Spanish rule. In 1578, the people of Amsterdam rose up against the papal forces and threw them from the city. Unfortunately, though, all thoughts of tolerance were forgotten and the zeal with which the Inquisition sought out Protestants was turned on Catholic worshippers. Their churches were violated, and they were forced to convert, or to worship in fearful secrecy. In 1579, seven provinces north of the Rhine concluded the Treaty of Utrecht, releasing the suffocating grip of Spanish rule. Although William was murdered in 1584, his sons continued his work, and in 1648 the treaties of the Hague and Westphalia organised the northern parts of the Low Countries into the United Provinces.

The Coming of the Golden Age

As Spanish influence faded, the Dutch star began to rise. First, they drew up agreements with the Portuguese, who had concluded trade treaties in the East that made them the sole source of goods such as spices and silks. Merchants from Amsterdam bought these goods and sold them in the north, making vast profits in the process.

When the Spanish took Portugal in 1580, the Amsterdam merchants decided to go into the import business themselves, and in 1595 sent their first fleet to Asia. In 1602 the United East India Company (VOC) was founded. It obtained a monopoly on all trade routes east of the Cape of Good Hope, founded a headquarters in Batavia (now Jakarta) in Java, and secured a monopoly trade agreement with Japan in 1641. VOC ships under the command of Abel Tasman landed in Australia some 150 years before Captain Cook.

Dutch ships brought back goods not seen before in the Western world: strange and wonderful creatures, new fruits and vegetables, and crafts of great beauty. They were all traded at immense profit with the other nations of Europe. The VOC became more powerful than many countries, Amsterdam was at the heart of this vast trading empire, and the Netherlands entered the period known as the 'Golden Age'.

Rich merchants needed banks and a financial infrastructure, which developed quickly in the city. People flooded in to take advantage of the new commercial opportunities, the population rose rapidly, and the old

Dutch West Indies

The Dutch looked west as well as east, and in 1609 sent Englishman Henry Hudson to search for a route to China. In the event, he traded with the native peoples of Manhattan Island (and named the Hudson River), travelled to the Caribbean, and took several islands as Dutch colonies.

medieval city simply could not cope. It was still contained within the boundaries set almost 150 years before. Plans were made for a series of three new canals – Herengracht, Keizersgracht and Prinsengracht – to form a girdle around the old medieval horseshoe. Canalside lots were sold to the wealthy who built the finest houses they could afford, but because canal frontage was expensive, the houses were narrow and deep.

The confidence of the city brought opportunities for the burgeoning arts and sciences. The artists Rembrandt, Frans Hals, Vermeer and Paulus Potter were all working in this era, their work much in demand by the merchant classes. At the same time, the Guild of Surgeons was learning about the physiology of the body at their meeting-place in the Waag, helped by Antonie van Leeuwenhoek who had invented the microscope.

Decline and Fall

Expansion quickly peaked, however, and the European powers who had carved up the New World set about testing each other in dynastic conflicts and colonial rivalry. The British were the main rivals of the Dutch on the high seas, and there

Tulip Mania

The first tulips were grown in the Netherlands in 1596 by the botanist Carolus Clusius at the botanical garden of the University of Leiden. These beautiful, colourful flowers were an instant hit – so much so that the first batch of bulbs was stolen. Early in the 17th century, as the economy experienced boom times during Amsterdam's Golden Age, wealthy merchants began to speculate in tulip bulbs, and prices for them rose to ridiculous levels. In 1637 three bulbs changed hands for a price that would have paid for a luxury canalside house. Tulipomania it was called, and it was bound to wither. When suddenly it did, not long after this high point, it drove a number of fortunes into the ground.

were several wars between the two in the 17th and 18th centuries. In 1667 the Dutch sailed up the River Medway and sank the British fleet moored at Chatham.

During the 18th century Amsterdam grew into the world's foremost financial centre, but the seeds of decline had already been planted. When the British colonies in New England

Vermeer's *Kitchen Maid* (c.1658)

rose up in revolt against the British, they found ready allies in the Dutch. From their colonies in the Caribbean they sent caches of arms and ammunition. The British were furious and went to war in 1780, destroying the Dutch Navy and precipitating a sudden decline in power and influence from which the Netherlands never recovered. Trade suffered to such an extent that in 1791 the VOC went into liquidation.

There were anti-Orange demonstrations by pro-French factions in the country, and in 1795 revolutionary France took the Netherlands. Under the yoke of another foreign power and with trade at an all-time low, the Golden Age was truly over.

The Return of the House of Orange

In 1806, Louis Bonaparte was installed by his brother as King of Holland and chose to make the fine Town Hall on the Dam his palace – now the Koninklijk Paleis. But Louis' secret trade links with Britain and his easy-going attitude to his subjects displeased Napoleon, and in 1810 the Emperor forced his brother to abdicate and annexed his kingdom to France. When Napoleon's bubble burst and French power

WILHELM KAREL HENDRIK ERISO
PRINS VAN ORANIE EN NASSAU
ERFSTADHOUDER CAPITEYN GENERAAL
EN ADMIRAEL VANDE SEVEN PROVINCIEN
DER VEREENIGDE NEDERLANDEN &c &c &c.

William of Orange

began to wane, William of Orange emerged from exile and was proclaimed king in 1813. Amsterdam had to work its way out of economic decline, but throughout the 19th century the city grew steadily.

Industrialisation changed the city. With the 1889 opening of Centraal Station, built over the old harbour wall, Amsterdam turned its back on its seafaring past and looked forward towards the mechanical age. Some of the oldest canals in the city centre were filled in to allow better access to motorised vehicles. The Dam was landlocked for the first time in its history. However, in the spirit of the Victorian Age, the philanthropic city fathers funded the building of several major museums and parks, along with instigating social reforms that created one of the first welfare states.

The 20th Century

The Netherlands stayed neutral in World War I, and efforts in the first half of the century were concentrated on land reclamation that increased agricultural production and living space. The Zuiderzee was finally tamed with the building of a 30-km (19-mile) dyke, the Afsluitdijk, in the north, creating a freshwater lake called the IJsselmeer. In the depression of the early 1930s there were several schemes to reduce unemployment, including the creation of the Amsterdamse Bos, a park and woodland on the outskirts of the city.

The Dutch hoped to remain neutral at the outbreak of World War II, but the Germans had other ideas and occupied the Low Countries in 1940. Amsterdammers were horrified at the treatment of their Jewish neighbours, and the dock workers staged a brave one-day strike to protest, but almost all the Jews were transported to concentration camps, never to return.

In September 1944, Operation Market Garden, made famous in the film *A Bridge Too Far*, saw thousands of allied paratroops dropping into the Netherlands to try to take key bridges on rivers leading to Germany. The Dutch welcomed them and provided support, but the operation was only a partial success. The Germans punished the Dutch people during the winter of 1944–45. Food and fuel were withdrawn, leaving the population to starve.

The Modern State

Soon after the end of the war, Dutch colonies in the Far East gained their independence – principally as the new nation of Indonesia – while the Netherlands sought to rebuild its shattered infrastructure. The Dutch used this period to consolidate their social systems to the benefit of the whole community. Amsterdam became a mecca for counter-culture groups such as hippies, who were drawn by the well-known open-mindedness of the people.

'People power' began to exert its influence, which ensured that, in Amsterdam at least, progress did not mean sweeping away the past. Where developers saw the opportunity to demolish derelict canal houses and warehouses, the people fought (sometimes literally) to save what they considered their heritage *(see pages 9–10)*. Today much of the historic city is protected by statute, although any redevelopment provokes much debate. The building of the Muziektheater and

Stadhuis in the 1980s, resulting in the demolition of several old houses, was a case in point, with vitriolic demonstrations by local pressure groups.

The Dutch joined the European Union (then the European Economic Community) in 1957, seeing it as a way of increasing their security and their economic stability. Their natural strengths in agricultural production and trade have ensured their success in the new alliance, and the Netherlands has become an important base for foreign companies who have trade ties in Europe. Throughout the 1990s the Dutch were at the forefront of a movement to open national borders, increase people's freedom of movement and expand trade within the EU, taking full part in the negotiations that surrounded the launch of the Euro currency in 1999. (In 2005, however, the Netherlands voted against the proposed EU constitution.)

Amsterdam has become one of the premier tourist cities in the world, trading on its historic centre and its wealth of artistic collections. Today it operates much as it did in the Golden Age with banking, trade, and modern 'pilgrims' (in the form of tourists) to ensure that it remains a wealthy city.

Tradition is still remembered in Amsterdam

Perhaps the only major spectre in the air is the one that worried the inhabitants of old Amstelredamme centuries ago: water levels. Global warming over the next few decades threatens to raise sea levels around the world, and the Netherlands – 'nether' means 'low-lying' or 'below' – will have to work very hard at solving the problem for the country's future inhabitants.

Historical Landmarks

c.1200 Wooden houses built at mouth of Amstel. The river is dammed.

1275 Count Floris V of Holland grants 'Amstelredamme' the rights to carry cargoes on the river toll-free.

1345 The 'Miracle of Amsterdam', basis of the Stille Omgang procession.

1419 Philip of Burgundy rises to power, unifying the Low Countries.

1452 Fire destroys wooden buildings; new ones to be of brick or stone.

1516 Spain under Charles V rules the Netherlands.

1567 Spain outlaws Calvinism: ruthless repression of Protestants.

1578 The Alteration: Protestants take control of Amsterdam.

1600–1700 The Golden Age: a Dutch empire built on trade with the East. Canal building in Amsterdam. The arts reach a high point.

1791 The United East India Company goes into liquidation.

1795 Revolutionary France occupies the Netherlands.

1813 The House of Orange returns to power.

1889 Centraal Station opened.

1940 Neutral Netherlands invaded by German forces.

1944–5 The Winter of Hunger.

1949 Indonesia gains independence from the Netherlands.

1960s 'People power' saves parts of historic Amsterdam from re-development. Amsterdam becomes home to minority groups.

1975 Demonstrations over plans to demolish parts of Nieuwmarkt.

1986 The 'Stopera' (Stadhuis and Opera) complex is completed.

1999 Renovation and expansion of the Van Gogh Museum.

2002 Crown Prince Willem Alexander marries Máxima Zorreguieta.

2003 Most of the Rijksmuseum closes for renovation.

2004 Stedelijk Museum closes for renovation; reopens in temporary premises. A branch of St Petersburg's Hermitage opens. After making a film critical of Islam, director Theo van Gogh is murdered in Amsterdam; anti-Muslim violence breaks out.

2006 The OV-chipkaart smart card begins to take over as the public transport 'ticket'.

2007 Centraal Station undergoes lengthy rebuilding and expansion.

WHERE TO GO

Amsterdam is a small city and eminently walkable, but if you only have a short time, take advantage of the tram system, which can transport you efficiently to all the most important attractions. Perhaps the most disconcerting thing for the newcomer is how to find your way around. The centre of Amsterdam can seem at first like a maze of tiny streets and canals with no overall plan. But think of it as a large spider's web, and once you understand the structure of the town, it is relatively easy to get around. The central core, around the square called the Dam, is horseshoe-shaped, and consists of a series of wide streets (the main one is Damrak/Rokin which cuts through the centre) and narrow alleys. It also has some of the oldest waterways, once so important for the delivery of goods from around the Dutch trading world.

> ## I amsterdam Card
>
> To make the most of your trip, the VVV (tourist board) sells an I amsterdam Card giving free or reduced-price access to museums, canal cruises and public transport. You'll also get discounts on bike hire and even on meals at certain restaurants. A one-day card costs €33, a two-day card €43 and a three-day card €53 (2007 rates). Cards can be bought from VVV offices in Amsterdam or in advance from Dutch tourist offices abroad.

This area is ringed by a girdle of canals (*grachten*), the major ones running outward in ever larger circles. Singel was once the outer barrier for medieval Amstelredamme, but as the city expanded, Herengracht (Gentlemen's Canal), Keizersgracht (Emperor's Canal) and Prinsengracht (Princes' Canal)

Traditional canalside architecture

Cycling along Brouwersgracht

enlarged the web. If you ever feel confused when strolling around town, remember that these three canals spread outwards in alphabetical order: H, K and P.

Small streets *(straatjes)* radiate out from the centre, crossing the canals by means of the thousand-plus bridges, which are such a distinctive part of the city landscape. To the north of the city centre, the IJ waterway becomes the IJsselmeer (a former inlet of the North Sea, now dammed); west of the IJ at this point is the Noordzeekanal, Amsterdam's present-day route to the open sea.

This guide divides the city into four sections that are easy to follow on foot. We start in the centre of the city, where you will be able to get your bearings, obtain whatever information you need from the VVV tourist information office *(see pages 28 and 128–9)* and take a **canal boat tour** – one of the best ways to get an overview of historic Amsterdam and to admire the true beauty of the city *(see page 117)*.

THE CENTRE

Central Amsterdam – once the medieval city – is very small indeed. The port was the lifeblood of the city at that time and ships would sail right into the heart of Amstelredamme, as it was known. Only a few architectural gems are left to remind us of this era, but the tangle of narrow alleyways gives a feel of the hustle and bustle that must have surrounded the traders.

Stationsplein to Damrak

The decision to locate **Centraal Station** on the site of the old harbour wall was the final death-knell of maritime trade for the city. It stopped large cargo ships from landing their cargoes and diminished the importance of the canal systems.

The station, opened in 1889, dominates the view up Damrak. The grand building was designed by P.J.H. Cuypers, who was also responsible for the design of the Rijksmuseum, and sits on three artificial islands supported by 8,687 wooden piles; it is currently undergoing extensive restoration and expansion.

East of the station, the TPG Building at Oosterdokskade 3–5 is, until the end of 2009, the temporary home of the city's modern art collection, the **Stedelijk Museum CS** (Municipal Museum; open daily 10am–6pm; admission charge;

Lean Times

As you stroll along the canalsides you'll notice that there are few houses standing absolutely upright – in fact, some seem to stand at a precarious angle. Don't assume that the buildings lean because of subsidence; most were designed to tilt towards the canal so that goods could be winched to the upper floors without crashing into the side of the house. Unfortunately, some houses tilted too much, resulting in the 1565 building code, which limited the inclination to 1 in 25.

Oudezijds Voorburgwal bridge
and Sint-Nicolaaskerk beyond

<www.stedelijk.nl>). Its regular base at Museum-plein is closed for renovation and extension. The museum's permanent collection includes pieces by Marc Chagall, Picasso, Monet, Cézanne and Matisse. There is also a comprehensive examination of the art and design movement known as De Stijl (The Style), which swept through the Netherlands just after World War I. But the museum warns that the classic modern highlights from its permanent collection might not be on show.

Close by, on the newly redeveloped waterside peninsula north of Piet Heinkade, stands the landmark **Muziekgebouw aan 't IJ** (Music Building on the IJ). It opened in 2005 and complements the classical emphasis of the Concertgebouw by focusing mainly on modern music.

Back at **Stationsplein**, in front of the station, is one of the city's three **VVV Amsterdam Tourist Offices** (tel: 551 2525; open daily 9am–5pm). It is housed in the Noord-Zuid Koffiehuis (or Smits Koffiehuis), dating from 1919, which was rebuilt in 1981 from the preserved pieces of the original, having been dismantled when the Metro was constructed in 1972. You will also find canal tour boats moored here and thousands of bicycles waiting for riders.

Walk across the square towards the city and, on the canal bridge, you will see on your left the distinctive spires of **Sint-Nicolaaskerk** (Saint Nicholas Church; open Mon–Sat 11am–4pm; free). This Catholic church, completed in 1887, replaced many of the secret chapels that were built for worship during the period of Catholic persecution. Once over the bridge you will be on **Damrak**. This wide boulevard was formerly a major docking area for ships from the colonies. On the left is a dock for glass-topped tour boats and beyond, at the head of Damrak, is the **Beurs van Berlage** (open generally Tues–Sun 11am–5pm, but exhibition hours vary; admission charge), the old stock exchange. Its refined modern lines were a revelation when it opened in 1903. Unfortunately, it didn't excite traders and is now used as a concert and exhibition hall featuring everything from chamber music to modern art.

Oude Kerk

The warren of streets to the left of the Beurs building is what Amsterdammers call **Oude Zijde** (Old Side). This was the old warehouse district in medieval times. The narrow alleyways

The late Gothic nave of the Oude Kerk dates from c.1300

The Red Light District is one of the liveliest areas after dark

are darker than in modern parts of the city and the houses even narrower and taller. Dominating the streets is the imposing Gothic **Oude Kerk** (Old Church; open Mon–Sat 11am–5pm, Sun 1–5pm; tower: Sat–Sun 1–5pm; admission charge).

The Oude Kerk is the oldest parish church in Amsterdam; work began in the early 13th century when Amstelredamme was a new trading town. Over the next three centuries, the church underwent several extensions until it took on the unusual shape it has today, with several chapels adding gables to the original structure. In the early days it acted as a marketplace and a hostel for the poor.

Inside, the scale of the church is impressive. Commemorative tombstones cover the floor, including that of Saskia, Rembrandt's wife. The stained-glass windows are glorious. One, commemorating the Peace of Munster, shows a Spanish official handing over the charter recognising the independent Dutch State. Opposite the Oude Kerk, is a step-gabled, baroque Dutch Renaissance house, **De Gecroonde Raep** (The Crowned Turnip), dating from 1615.

The Red Light District

The northern reaches of the canalside streets Oudezijds Voorburgwal and Oudezijds Achterburgwal, southwest of the Oude Kerk, are home to Amsterdam's infamous **Red Light District**, known as the Wallen or 'walls', or the Walletjes or 'little walls'. As in any large port, prostitution has always been rife and, although some Calvinists tried to stamp it out, it still thrives today. In modern Amsterdam the industry has been legitimised and regulated in an attempt to curb the most disturbing facets of exploitation and to address health concerns. Prostitutes in the Netherlands are entitled to regular health checks and are expected to pay taxes on their earnings – a typically pragmatic Dutch solution to a social issue.

The area is safe (except perhaps in the early hours of the morning) and usually busy with tourists. The tree-lined canals and old, narrow iron bridges are some of the prettiest in the city, and most prostitutes ply their trade behind relatively discreet windows, not on the streets.

Sex and Drugs

Perhaps Amsterdam's most widely publicised acts of tolerance in recent history have been in the areas of the sex industry and drug-taking. Amsterdammers have looked at feasible and practical responses to the issues, and decriminalised some aspects of both. This does not make the city one big den of iniquity, and these areas are still controlled and regulated; in fact, you could visit Amsterdam and be quite unaware of these activities. There's just a recognition here that, provided no harm comes to you or others around you, then you should be free, as an adult, to make your own choices.

At ground level, there are shops – seedy, eye-catching or amusing, depending on your point of view, selling sex wares and attracting customers. But don't get too distracted, or you'll miss the rows of dainty gables, quirky wall plaques and window boxes brimming with flowers, which give the whole area a cheery feel. Don't be surprised to find offices, shops and restaurants side by side with the brothels here – it's all part of Amsterdam life. At night the streets come alive with bars, clubs and adult shows and it becomes one of the liveliest parts of the city. Make sure you stay on the busier, well-lit thoroughfares on your way back to your hotel.

Museum Het Amstelkring

You will find several historical gems as you wander the Wallen. One of the narrow houses on Oudezijds Voorburgwal (No. 40) has a wonderful secret to share. **Museum Het Amstelkring**

Chinatown is full of small shops selling quirky wares

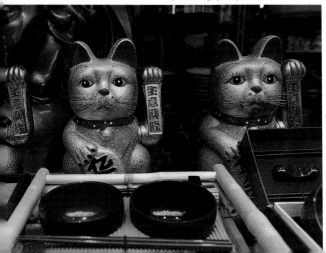

(open Mon–Sat 10am–5pm, Sun and hols 1–5pm; admission charge) was a merchant's house bought by the Catholic Jan Hartman in 1661. Following the 'Alteration' in 1578, Catholics were not permitted to practise their religion, so Hartman, along with a number of other wealthy Catholics of the time, had a secret chapel built for family worship. Although they were common at the time, this is

A rare sign, forbidding bicyles, in Amsterdam's Chinatown

now the only complete secret chapel left in the city, and because of its location, the house is called *Ons' Lieve Heer op Solder* (Our Lord in the Attic). Three additional houses were added to create extra space, and several of the other rooms are furnished in 18th-century style. It is a fascinating glimpse of a difficult time in Amsterdam's history, but it's not just a museum piece – it is still used for weddings. A few doors along from the Amstelkring is the Dutch Renaissance **D'Leeuwenburg Huis**, a restored step-gabled house dating from 1605.

De Waag

Southeast of the Oude Kerk you can walk through the small Chinese Quarter to reach **De Waag**. One of the oldest buildings in the city, it opened in 1488 as a city gate to mark the eastern boundary of the city along the new wall built after the disastrous fire in the 1450s. The numerous turrets and rounded tower give it the look of a fairytale castle but it has had a more colourful history. Public executions were held here in the 16th century, with the condemned being kept in a small cell on the ground floor before they met their fate.

The Zuiderkerk's soaring spire

From the early 17th century it became the weigh house *(waaggebouw)* for cargoes entering or leaving the city down the Geldersekade canal to the north. The upper floors were used by trades' guilds for meetings and by the Guild of Surgeons for practical medical research, including experiments with cadavers. Two of Rembrandt's most celebrated paintings, *The Anatomy Lesson of Dr Deijman* and *The Anatomy Lesson of Dr Tulp* were commissioned by the Guild of Surgeons and originally hung in the Waag. In the early 19th century the weigh house closed, and the Waag had a number of less illustrious tenants. It now houses a superb café-restaurant, In de Waag, so you can stop for refreshment and admire the Gothic interior at the same time.

Nieuwmarkt and Zuiderkerk

Nieuwmarkt (New Market) surrounds the Waag and is home to several different types of market throughout the week. If you walk to the north side of the Waag and look along Geldersekade you will see a tower dominating the skyline. This is the **Schreierstoren**, which is also part of the new city wall of 1480. City scholars are divided as to the reason for the tower's name. Some say it comes from the word *schreien*, which means 'weeping', as it was a place where sailors' distressed wives came to wave their men off to sea. Others claim that the name is a derivation of the word *scherpe* (sharp), describing the tower's position on a 90-degree bend in the wall.

From the Waag walk down Sint-Antoniesbreestraat, past modern apartment blocks built in the 1970s. Look out for the magnificent **De Pintohuis** at No. 69, a mansion bought by wealthy Jewish merchant Isaäc de Pinto in 1651, and rebuilt by his son David Emanuel to more or less its present look in 1686.

Off the right side of Sint-Antoniesbreestraat is the ornate tower of the **Zuiderkerk** (South Church; open Mon–Fri 9am–4pm, Sat noon–4pm; free; tower: Apr–Sept Tues–Sun 1–5pm; admission charge). Begun in 1603, this was the first Protestant place of worship to be built after the Reformation. Designed by Hendrick de Keyser, its lines were much admired by Sir Christopher Wren. It was deconsecrated in 1929 and is now a community information centre.

At the end of Sint-Antoniesbreestraat is a tiny square with a wonderful view along Oudeschans to your left. You'll find an old house, now a small bar/café, in the foreground and

Rembrandt's Inspiration

Rembrandt van Rijn had a passion for collecting rare or precious objects. This desire played a part in his downfall, but his collection at the Rembrandthuis (see page 36) tells us much about Dutch society in the 1600s. Beautiful man-made items from the Dutch colonies sit beside Roman and Greek sculptures from the classical era. There are a number of globes, indicating the expansion of the known world in Rembrandt's time, seashells and strange stuffed beasts from far-off lands, and etchings by Raphael, Titian and Holbein, kept in heavy leather-bound books, showing new visual styles in form and colour. Inspiration was rich indeed in 17th-century Amsterdam.

The Polders

Some 6,500 sq km (2,500 sq miles) of the Netherlands has been reclaimed from the sea. This was achieved by building dykes along the coast, rivers and canals, and pumping the ground water to the far side of the dyke to dry out the land. Many areas of Amsterdam, such as Vondelpark, are 2m (6½ft) below sea level and Schiphol Airport is 4.5m (14½ft) below sea level.

the **Montelbaanstoren** behind. Built as part of a new outer defensive wall in 1512, the tower originally had a flat roof – the ornate peak that gives it such panache was added by Hendrick de Keyser in 1606. Today it is used by the local water authority as an office building.

Rembrandt's House

After pausing to take a photograph, cross the street to Jodenbreestraat (Jewish Broad Street) and the three-storey brick building with red shutters. This is the **Museum Het Rembrandthuis** (Rembrandt's House; open daily 10am–5pm; admission charge; <www.rembrandthuis.nl>), which was home to the great artist from 1639 to 1660. Rembrandt bought the house as he rose in prestige and wealth. He created a studio on the top floor, where there was abundant natural light to illuminate his subjects, and sufficient space for him to teach his numerous pupils. The painter lived with his wife and their young son on the first floor. Unfortunately, he was not able to live out his life in his home. His lack of financial acumen and love of expensive objects brought him to bankruptcy in 1656 and he had to sell all his possessions, including the house, in 1660.

The whole house was restored in the late 1990s, including the studio and the painter's *kunstkamer* or art cabinet, to re-create the early 1600s as faithfully as possible. More than 250 of the artist's etchings are beautifully presented around the upper floors of the house.

THE SOUTHEAST

Waterlooplein

Parallel to Jodenbreestraat, on its left-hand side, is **Waterlooplein**, named after the famous battle and home to a flea market of the same name. Every day (except Sunday) you'll find an eclectic mix of second-hand crockery, clothing and electricals on sale, along with cotton clothes from India or Indonesia.

The eastern end of the market square is dominated by the twin spires of **Mozes en Aäronkerk** (Moses and Aaron Church), a Catholic church built in 1840 on the site of a secret chapel. The Old Testament figures of Moses and Aaron were found depicted on gable stones in the original building and were set into the wall of the new edifice. The fine towers are actually wood rather than stone. They were painted to match the sandstone walls in a 1990 restoration.

The flea market at Waterlooplein is the oldest in Amsterdam

The picturesque Magere Brug

Waterlooplein, and its market, used to be much larger, but a massive building project, begun in the early 1980s, reduced its size considerably. Protesters deplored the loss of several old canal houses fringing the square, which constituted much of what was left of the old Jewish Quarter. In the 1980s squatters battled against riot police and water cannons. Nevertheless, the construction went ahead, and the result of this labour is the **Muziektheater** and **Stadhuis**, sitting majestically on the River Amstel. Opened in 1986, the attractive glass-fronted building is home to the Netherlands Opera and National Ballet and hosts a range of travelling companies in the largest auditorium in the country.

At one end of Waterlooplein is a black marble memorial commemorating Jewish Resistance fighters from World War II.

Towards Magere Brug

The **River Amstel** has always been a major artery through the city and even today you will see a large amount of commercial traffic passing along the waterway. From the terrace and walkway around the Muziektheater there are wonderful views of the boats and the canal houses bordering the water. The bridge in front of the Muziektheater provides a wonderful view down the river and is also one of the most interesting bridges in Amsterdam. The **Blauwbrug** (Blue Bridge) is named after the colour of the previous bridge that occupied the site. The present bridge, dating from 1880, is based on Pont Alexandre III in Paris and is ornamented with carvings of ships and other maritime themes.

A block upstream from the Blauwbrug on the east (right) bank is the neoclassical Amstelhof (1681), a former nursing home. Since 2004, the Neerlandia Building, an annexe of the Amstelhof, with an entrance on Nieuwe Herengracht, has been the site of **Hermitage Amsterdam** (open daily 10am–5pm; admission charge), a branch of St Petersburg's State Hermitage Museum. In coming years, the rest of the Amstelhof will fill up with elements from the mother museum's vast collection.

Although the Blauwbrug is the most ornate bridge in the city, Amsterdammers and visitors alike have a soft spot for its neighbour a little way south down the Amstel, **Magere Brug** or 'Skinny Bridge'. This white, wooden drawbridge is picture-perfect and one of the most enduring symbols of the

The Skinny Sisters

How did Magere Brug get its name? *Mager* means 'skinny' in Dutch, and it would be simple to assume that its name refers to the narrowness of the bridge. Not so, say Amsterdammers, who will regale you with stories of two sisters called Mager who each had a house on opposite sides of the bridge and who paid for the original bridge to be built. By amazing coincidence, these two sisters were also thin, which prompts comments about the '*mager* Mager sisters'.

Since the word *mager* ('mah-khur') is extremely difficult for non-Dutch speakers to pronounce authentically, one does wonder whether these stories may just be a way for Amsterdammers to poke a little friendly fun as visitors struggle with the language.

city. It is even prettier at dusk when the lights on its arches and spars are switched on. There has been a bridge here since the 1670s but the present one was erected only in 1969.

Along the river on either side of Magere Brug are a number of old barges moored along the banks. The large craft, which would once have carried heavy cargoes such as grain and coal, now make surprisingly large, comfortable, quirky and very expensive homes. Beyond Magere Brug on the east bank of the Amstel you will see the façade of the **Koninklijk Theater Carré**. Traditionally the site of the Carré Circus, this was where the Carré family had a wooden building erected to house their shows. Later the authorities deemed this structure to be a fire hazard and so the Carrés had this beautiful stone building designed for them, which opened for performances in 1887. It now hosts many different types of performance, but a circus always appears here at Christmas time.

The Golden Age kitchen in the Museum Willet-Holthuysen

Herengracht

Cross the river via Magere Brug then travel one block north and take a left along the northern bank of **Herengracht**. Here, you will get your first look at the canal system that was built during Amsterdam's Golden Age,

Watch your step!

Wear comfortable shoes when you explore the city: uneven surfaces can be hard on the feet – especially the cobbled canalside roads, which are made even more irregular by tree roots.

revolutionising the city. During its time, this was probably the most sought-after, expensive real estate in the world.

Herengracht particularly has many beautiful houses, which can only really be appreciated by strolling past them. This part of town is still mostly residential, and many houses have been converted into apartments for successful Amsterdammers. It is fascinating to peek inside at the ultra-modern interiors, which give a feel of the flair the Dutch have for interior design.

Museum Willet-Holthuysen

At No. 605 Herengracht, the **Museum Willet-Holthuysen** (open Mon–Fri 10am–5pm, Sat–Sun and holidays 11am–5pm; admission charge) gives you the opportunity to look behind the façade of a genuine Golden Age house. It was completed in 1687 and structurally has changed very little since that time, although it has been altered cosmetically several times as fashions changed.

In 1855 it came into the possession of the Holthuysen family. Gerard Holthuysen was a successful trader in glass and English coal. After the death of Gerard and his wife, the house was inherited by their daughter Louisa who later married Abraham Willet. He had a love of art and was a founding member of the Royal Antiquarian Society, whose aim was to promote national art and history.

On her death in 1895, Louisa bequeathed the house and its contents to the city of Amsterdam on the one condition that it would be opened as a museum. This it duly was in 1896, and today you can examine in detail the furniture, porcelain and numerous artworks that had been collected by the family over many years.

Museum Van Loon and Reguliersgracht

Continue south a short way towards Keizersgracht to No. 672, the **Museum Van Loon** (open Wed–Mon 11am–5pm; admission charge), a canal-side residence dating from 1672. Its elegant interior includes portraits from generations of the influential Van Loon family and, in the ornamental garden, there is a coach house in the style of a Greek temple.

Rembrandt looks down on the square that bears his name

Travel further along Herengracht to the end of the second block. Here you will find one of the most fascinating views of the canal ring. From the bridge at **Reguliersgracht** it is possible to see 14 other bridges by looking up and down Herengracht and ahead down the adjoining Reguliersgracht (this view is even better at water level, so take a canal cruise – and your camera – *see page 117*). Reguliersgracht has some very pretty houses and is quieter than the main three 'girdle' canals which were built at the same time.

Thorbeckeplein and Rembrandtplein

The small square here is **Thorbeckeplein**, where you will see a suitably sombre statue of Johan Rudolf Thorbecke who designed the Dutch Constitution in 1848. Wander through the square, which is the scene of an art market on Sundays, to reach **Rembrandtplein**, one of the city's most vibrant social centres. This square was formerly called Botermarkt (a butter market was held here in the 19th century) but it was renamed when the large statue of Rembrandt was sited here in 1878.

One wonders what the artist would have made of the square, since it now busy with theatres, cinemas, clubs, show halls, bars and restaurants – and dominated by vibrant neon signs. On a summer evening, however, it is a wonderful place to sit with a drink and watch the world go by.

The Jewish Quarter

Beyond the eastern end of Waterlooplein you will see the Mr Visserplein, busy with several lanes of traffic. Head across the square to Weesperstraat and Jonas Daniël Meijerplein to find the **Joods Historisch Museum** (Jewish Historical Museum; open daily 11am–5pm; admission charge; <www.jhm.nl>), which documents the history of the once large and influential Jewish community in the city. Jewish history in Amsterdam dates back to the late 16th century, but was cut short by the Nazi occupation of the city that began in 1940.

The systematic deportation of the Jewish population to concentration camps tore the community apart, and

Explore Jewish culture at the Joods Historisch Museum

The 17th-century Portugees-Israëlietische Synagoge

after the war only a handful returned to their homes. The museum, which opened in 1987, was created by the amalgamation of four old Ashkenazi synagogue buildings. The exhibitions reveal the history of Amsterdam's Jewish community, explain the philosophies of Judaism and examine the wider issues of Jewish identity.

Across busy Weesperstraat are two other reminders of the once thriving Jewish community. In a stark, exposed position near the road in Jonas Daniël Meijerplein, is the **Dokwerker Statue** by Mari Andriessen. This figure of a working man commemorates the day in February 1941 when the dock workers rose up in protest against the Nazi deportation of the Jews. Behind the statue is the **Portugees-Israëlietische Synagoge** (Portuguese Synagogue; open Apr–Oct Sun–Fri 10am–6pm, Nov–Mar Sun–Thur 10am–6pm, Fri 10am–3pm; admission charge), which was inaugurated in 1675 for the Spanish and Portuguese Sephardic Jews who settled in the city. Its design is said to be based on that of King Solomon's Temple.

The Plantage

From Jonas Daniël Meijerplein look southeast to the glass houses of the **Hortus Botanicus** (Botanical Garden; open Apr–Oct Mon–Fri 9am–5pm, Sat–Sun 11am–5pm, Nov–Mar till 4pm; admission charge), easily seen just across the Nieuwe Herengracht. Cross the canal by walking left along its banks to the nearby bridge. Once across, you have entered the Plantage area of the city, formerly an area of parkland but developed from the mid-19th century into one of the first of Amsterdam's suburbs.

The Botanical Garden has a long and illustrious history. It began as a small medicinal garden in 1682, but soon became the depository for many of the new plant species brought from Dutch colonies in the Golden Age, and was responsible for developing each genus for cultivation, propagation and commercial exploitation. The distinctive glass houses were added in 1912, and today the gardens have one of the largest collections in the world.

A two-minute walk down Plantage Middenlaan leads you to **Artis** (open May–Oct daily 9am–6pm, Sat till sunset; Nov–Apr daily 9am–5pm; admission charge; <www.artis.nl>), a fascinating complex of zoo, aquarium, planetarium and geological museum, which aims to increase your knowledge of the physical world. The zoo was one of the first in Europe when it

Canal views from the Hortus Botanicus

Tropenmuseum

opened its doors in 1838, and it has continued as a ground-breaking institution, now acting as a centre for efforts to save several endangered species of animals. Many of the old, confined Victorian enclosures where specimens were kept, were re-developed in the 1990s to create a more pleasant environment for the animals. The **Planetarium** and other areas of Artis offer many fun ways for all to learn about the world around us.

Tropenmuseum

Southeast of Artis, across two canals and busy roads, is **Oosterpark**, an open green area with a lake and play areas (take tram No. 9 or 14 rather than walking here from the city centre). In the northern corner of the park is the **Tropen-museum** (open daily 10am–5pm; admission charge; <www.tropenmuseum.nl>), once the home of the Dutch Colonial Institute. The building was constructed in 1926 to house the institute's collection of artefacts from the tropics. Today, the aim of the museum is to improve our knowledge of the world's tropical areas and promote an understanding of the peoples in these developing parts of the world. A vast collection of artefacts from the former Dutch East Indies (now Indonesia) was the starting point for the displays, which range from tribal masks to tools and utensils. Recreations of a Bombay street and Arab souk, among other locales, bring home the reality of life in different societies. The museum also has a **Tropenmuseum Junior** (Children's Museum; tel: 568 8233) offering 6- to 13-year-olds a chance to explore the collection and interact with the exhibits. Special guides show children the artefacts and explain their context. The Junior museum tour must be booked in advance, and at present are in Dutch only.

Entrepotdok

North of Artis is **Entrepotdok**, which, in the 19th century, was the warehouse region of the city with carefully designed canals forming one of the busiest port areas in Europe. The warehouses fell into disrepair in the 20th century and lay empty for many years before they became a centre for the 1960s' and 1970s' squatter revolution that overtook the city. Since the 1980s, the area has been totally renovated and the

Amsterdam Street Addresses

A formal system of addresses with street names and numbers was only introduced to the city by the French in 1795. Before this, gable stones and wall plaques were used as a way of indicating either the purpose of a commercial building or of explaining the precise site of a home. Directions might have been something like 'three doors down from the Red Fox'. Some of these plaques have been left in place – look out for them as you stroll the banks of the canals.

warehouses gutted to create spacious modern housing, offices, and bars and restaurants without changing the basic design of the buildings.

Heading north, you will reach the main street, Prins Hendrikkade, which runs along the northern edge of the city (this takes you back to Centraal Station to the left). As you cross over the Nieuwe Vaart canal, look left for a glimpse of the only windmill left in the city's central area. The **De Gooyer windmill** was built in the early 18th century to grind corn. It now houses a small brewery, Brouwerij 't IJ, and a bar.

The Scheepvaartmuseum

Across the bridge, walk towards Kattenburgerplein and a large square building with a sailing ship docked outside. This is the **Scheepvaartmuseum** (Maritime Museum; closed for extensive renovation until 2009; <www.scheep vaartmuseum.nl>). The building housing the museum was built in 1656 for the Dutch Navy, and its strong walls safeguarded a vast arsenal that once protected Dutch interests around the world. Its extensive exhibits document the long, illustrious history of maritime achievement of the Dutch, with paintings, maps and maritime models explaining the part that ships – and particularly those of the VOC (United East India Company) – played in the growth of the empire in the 17th century.

NEMO Science Centre

Next to the museum, and recognisable by its vast bulk and huge green outer walls, is the **NEMO Science Centre** (open Tues–Sun 10am–5pm, daily in school holidays; admission charge; <www.e-nemo.nl>). Designed by architect Renzo Piano, and opened in 1997, the centre was created to bring the latest science and technology literally into the hands of the lay person, whatever their age.

At the Scheepvaartmuseum

The location of the NEMO itself is a technological marvel. It sits high above the entrance to the IJ tunnel, which takes six lanes of traffic under the IJ waterway to Amsterdam's northern suburbs and beyond. Inside the centre you can try your hand at playing the stock exchange by computer, change the wheel on a car, or look at the cells of the body through a microscope. There are hands-on experiments for everyone from young children to adults, focusing on five linked themes: Energy, Humanity, Interactivity, Science and Technology.

Outside the museum is the re-creation of the United East India Company ship ***Amsterdam***, a life-size replica of a real ship completed in 1748. The ship is temporarily moored here whist the Scheepvaartmuseum is under restoration. The *Amsterdam* has a crew to man her. As you explore her decks, the captain will illustrate his course with charts of the time, the doctor will explain his rather primitive treatments, and the ordinary seamen will be happy to sing you a Dutch sea shanty.

THE SOUTHWEST

The southwest section takes on a fan shape from the centre of the city, widening as it travels out and taking in the major art museums.

Muntplein

Our starting point is **Muntplein**, at the junction of the River Amstel and the Singel canal. Although only a small square, and cut by numerous tramlines, it has a particularly beautiful tower – **Munttoren** (Mint Tower), originally a medieval gate guard-

Tulip bulbs of all kinds on sale at the Bloemenmarkt

ing the entrance to the city. It was damaged by fire in 1619, and the clock tower was added by Hendrick de Keyser during the renovations. In 1699 the carillon was installed and this still fills the air with its tinkling sounds. During the war with France in 1672, when Amsterdam's supply of money was cut off, the tower became the city mint, and the name has stuck. Just along the canal is the gruesome **Torture Museum** (open daily 10am–11pm; admission charge).

Bloemenmarkt

In the shadow of the tower and partly floating on the Singel (the medieval protective moat for the city) is

▶ the **Bloemenmarkt** (Flower Market). The daily market has been held for centuries, when the flower sellers would arrive by canal with boats laden with blooms. Today the stalls still float on barges permanently attached to the canal wall. The blooms they sell bring a splash of colour to even the dullest Amsterdam day.

Street musician in Leidseplein

Stroll along the market until you reach Koningsplein and take a left down Leidsestraat. This is a major shopping street and one of the busiest because it links one of the largest squares in the city to the central area. Stop at Metz & Co department store, which sits on the corner of Keizersgracht and Leidsegracht. One of the oldest shops in Amsterdam, it offers good views of the city from the café on the top floor.

Leidseplein

At the end of Leidsestraat is **Leidseplein**, the busiest square ◀ in the city, with bars and cafés spilling onto it; it's a major nightlife focus, too. Look out for a small grassy area, with sculptures of life-size iguanas and other large lizards. The narrow streets leading off the square are filled with cinemas, concert halls and intimate live venues. There is also a busy VVV Amsterdam Tourist Office *(see pages 129)* here.

In summer you will find several different street performers vying for your euros. It's a place where talented music students play classical pieces, or musicians from around the world play their traditional tunes, taking their turn with jugglers, mime artists and magicians. Whatever the time of year, as the sun sets, the neon lights are switched on, and people flock to enjoy the restaurants and nightclubs that keep the square buzzing until the early hours of the morning.

On the western side of Leidseplein you will find the **Stadsschouwburg** (Municipal Theatre), built in 1894. Once the premier opera house in the city, it has been usurped by the Muziektheater, but still hosts regular performances of visiting and Dutch theatre companies, being home to the Toneelgroep drama group. Across the square is the **American Hotel**, an art nouveau treasure and national monument completed in 1902. If you are not staying here you can visit the Café Américain on the ground floor to enjoy the sumptuous surroundings.

Vondelpark

Turn left after Leidseplein and across the Singel you will find the **Amsterdam Casino and Lido** on your left. On your right, across Stadhouderskade, is a narrow gate into **Vondelpark**. This park, founded in 1865, has been called 'the lungs of Amsterdam' and was founded after a number of philanthropic city fathers decided that there was a need for a genteel recreation area for the city's population, many of whom lived in overcrowded slums. The park was named after the Netherlands' premier poet and playwright Joost van den Vondel and designed in the English fashion of the times. It originally served as a private park, paid for by the wealthy families who lived around it. Today its 46 hectares (120 acres) have farm animals, flocks of parakeets, jogging tracks and cycle paths.

The large pavilion, which opened in 1881, is now the **Nederlands Filmmuseum** (open Mon–Fri 9am–10pm, Sat–Sun 4 or 5–10.15pm; admission charge for screenings; due to move to Amsterdam North in 2009). It shows more than 1,000 films each year, including outdoor screenings.

Museumplein

Only five minutes to the south of Leidseplein is the Museum Quarter, for many visitors the *raison d'être* for their visit to Amsterdam. Here, three of the most important art collections in Europe normally sit side by side, allowing visitors to walk from one to the next in a matter of moments. Although all very different in appearance, they are brought together by an open space which in the late 1990s was redesigned and replanted to accentuate the buildings. The square is called, not surprisingly, **Museumplein**.

Rijksmuseum

The highlight of any art lover's trip to Amsterdam would ordinarily be the **Rijksmuseum** (National Art Gallery; open Sat–Thur 9am–6pm, Fri 9am–10pm; admission charge), which is home to arguably the greatest collection of Dutch

Rijksmuseum

art in the world. However, most of the museum has been closed for renovation since late 2003, with the work due to continue until 2009. One section, the Philips Wing, remains open for the display of key works in the collection, under the title 'Rijksmuseum: The Masterpieces' some of which are detailed below. To check on progress and to find out what is on show, visit the museum's website, <www.rijksmuseum.nl>.

The Rijksmuseum is housed within a magnificent Victorian Gothic building, designed by P.J.H. Cuypers and opened in 1885. Additions were completed in 1898 and 1919. The collection is varied, but most visitors come to see the works of the Dutch masters from the 15th to the 17th century. Among the collection are 20 works by Rembrandt, including *The Night Watch*, properly entitled *The Company of Captain Frans Banning Cocq and Lieutenant Willem van Ruytenburch*. The work, which was commissioned by the company for its barracks, is remarkable for its lack of formality and very different from the accepted style of the day. Its size is impressive, yet the painting was originally even larger. It was moved to the Town Hall in 1715 but was too wide

Self-portrait of Rembrandt, painted in 1669

for the place that had been chosen to display it, so the canvas was trimmed to make it fit, totally removing three figures on the right side of the painting. Originally, the picture showed the two major subjects towards the left of the scene. Now they stand in the centre, altering for ever the original focus of Rembrandt's composition.

Johannes Vermeer is well represented, and his effective

Rembrandt's *The Night Watch*

use of light can be seen in *The Kitchen Maid*, painted *c.*1658–60 and now one of the gallery's best-loved pieces. There are paintings by Frans Hals, the founding artist of the Dutch School, along with a collection of Dutch artists who were influenced or schooled by the masters. Rembrandt was a prolific teacher and his pupils produced work so similar to his that later many were mistaken for the great artist's work.

Look out also for the painting by a lesser-known artist, Gerrit Adriaensz Berckheyde, of Herengracht in 1672 when its grand houses were being completed. The scene has no trees and shows the 'Gentleman's Canal' in pristine condition.

Works of later Dutch artists include a number by artists of the Hague School, which flourished in the late 1800s and whose best-known representative is Jan van Huysum. The museum also has a collection of work by non-Dutch artists, including Rubens, Tintoretto and El Greco, along with porcelain, furniture, sculpture and decorative arts, and Asiatic art.

Amsterdam's strikingly modern
Van Gogh Museum

Van Gogh Museum

Visible just behind the Rijks-museum are the modern lines of the **Van Gogh Museum** (open daily 10am–6pm, Fri till 10pm; admission charge; <www.vangogh museum.nl>), devoted to the work of the Dutch master Vincent van Gogh. The main building, by architect Gerrit Rietveld, opened in 1973; a separate circular wing, by Kisho Kurokawa, is used to host temporary exhibitions. The museum houses more than 200 paintings and 500 drawings by the painter, covering all periods of his troubled career. The bulk of the collection was collated by Vincent's brother Theo van Gogh, who also kept more than 800 letters written by his brother.

Vincent's working life was short but frenetic, interspersed with periods of manic depression, and his paintings reflect his moods. His 1885 work *The Potato Eaters* shows the hard lives endured by the rural poor among whom Van Gogh lived at this time. Contrast this with the superb vibrant colours of *The Bedroom in Arles* and *Vase with Sunflowers*, both painted after Vincent moved to Provence in 1888. Van Gogh is renowned for his reinterpretation of the works of other artists, and the museum has prime examples of works based on paintings by Rembrandt, Delacroix and Millet.

Stedelijk Museum and Surrounding Area

Next door to the Van Gogh Museum is the stately **Stedelijk Museum**, which was finished in 1895 (it is closed for renovation and extension until 2009 or later, with the collection on display at the temporary Stedelijk Museum CS quarters near Centraal Station; *see page 27*). The façade is neoclassical with figures of famous Dutch men such as the architect Hendrick de Keyser gazing down on the passing crowds. It was built specifically to house the private art collection of

Dutch Masters Old and New

The Golden Age of the Netherlands (roughly speaking, the 17th century) produced a number of brilliant artists who left a rich legacy of work. In the years since, there have been further shining lights.

Frans Hals (c.1580–1666) is considered the founder of the Dutch School of realistic painting. He introduced to fine art the captured moment – the glance or casual expression not formerly seen in formal portraits. His celebrated portrait *The Laughing Cavalier* is in the Rijksmuseum.

Rembrandt Harmenszoon van Rijn (1606–69). Today, the best known artist of the Dutch School, Rembrandt revolutionised painting with his informal composition and use of light. He lived in Amsterdam for much of his life. Some of his best work is in the Rijksmuseum and a collection of his sketches at his house (Het Rembrandthuis).

Johannes (Jan) Vermeer (1632–75) painted only around 30 works, but his attention to detail and sympathetic use of light later made his work famous. His *The Kitchen Maid* is in the Rijksmuseum.

Jacob van Ruisdael (c.1628–82). Master of the landscape, he had the ability to create an almost photographic realism. A number of his works are in the Rijksmuseum.

Vincent van Gogh (1853–90) developed his strong use of form and colour after he settled in Provence. Suffering from mental illness, he died after shooting himself just before his revolutionary work was recognised. The Van Gogh Museum has over 200 of his paintings.

Piet Mondrian (1872–1944) brought painting down to its essence, with stark abstract lines and blocks created using primary colours. Examples of his work can be viewed at the Stedelijk Museum.

Sophia de Bruyn, who then bequeathed it to the city in 1890. In 1938 it became the museum of modern art.

Diamond Territory

If you feel culturally exhausted after your 'museum-fest', the streets around Museumplein offer some exciting retail therapy. Walk across Paulus Potterstraat from the Van Gogh Museum and you will find **Coster Diamonds**, one of the oldest 'houses' in the city, where you can watch diamonds being polished and maybe buy a carat or two. Van Baerlestraat, bordering the west side of Museumplein, is the haute-couture area of the city. For further culture of a musical nature

the **Concertgebouw** on Van Baerlstraat is home to the orchestra of the same name. The main auditorium is considered to have almost perfect acoustics even though the designer of the building, Adolf Leonard van Gendt, had no experience in this specialised area.

Nieuwe Spiegelstraat and the Golden Bend

If you want to stroll back to town after your visit to the museums, then walk through the open courtyard that cuts through the centre of the Rijksmuseum, across Stadhouderskade and on to narrow Spiegelgracht and its continuation **Nieuwe Spiegelstraat**. This centre of antiques and art galleries has some wonderful windows to gaze into. Prices tend to be high, but the dealers are some of the most experienced in the world and they are sure to give you good advice.

Walk north along the whole length of Nieuwe Spiegelstraat and you will eventually reach Herengracht at its most spectacular point. When it was first dug, and the lots of land sold, it was soon realised that this section of the canal (between Vijzelstraat and Leidsestraat) would have the largest houses inhabited by the richest families in the city. For this reason it has become known as the **Golden Bend**. Many of these grand old buildings now house banks and financial institutions.

Along the Golden Bend

THE NORTHWEST

The Begijnhof

The northwest section abuts the centre, beginning at **Kalver-straat**, the rather brash, 'happening' shopping street which cuts the centre of Amsterdam from north to south. In a small square called **Spui** you will find a book market on Fridays. Off the north side of the square a narrow alleyway, Ge-dempte Begijnensloot, leads to the entrance of the **Begijnhof** (open daily 8am–1pm; free), a haven of tranquillity in the centre of the city.

The cluster of buildings around a small central square was set aside in 1346 for the benefit of the Beguines, members of a lay Catholic sisterhood. They lived simple lives and in return for their lodgings undertook to care for the sick and educate the poor. Although nothing remains of the 14th-century houses, No. 34 is **Het Houten Huys**, Amsterdam's oldest house, dating from around 1425.

The Catholic chapel dates from 1671 when it was built in a style designed to disguise its purpose. The spectacular stained-glass windows depict the Miracle of Amsterdam. In the centre of the courtyard is an earlier church now called the English Reformed Church. It was rented to English and Scottish worshippers in 1607 after the Alteration, and the Pilgrim Fathers worshipped here before they set off on their long journey to the New World (they came to Amsterdam from England before they set sail for America).

Smoking

It is difficult to find a no-smoking area in bars and cafés in Amsterdam.
A decision on whether to impose a smoking ban is to be taken in 2009.

The last Beguine died as recently as 1971 and today, although the houses are still offered only to single women of the Christian faith, the women are not expected to undertake lay work.

Stained-glass windows in the English Reformed Church

Amsterdam's Historical Museum

Behind the Begijnhof is the old Convent of St Lucy, which became the city orphanage after the Alteration, although it was open only to well-to-do orphans; the poor had to fend for themselves. It was extended several times, including a wing designed by Hendrick de Keyser, and opened in 1975 as the **Amsterdams Historisch Museum** (Amsterdam Historical Museum; open Mon–Fri 10am–5pm, Sat–Sun and holidays 11am–5pm; admission charge; <www.ahm.nl>). Its rooms reveal the details of the development of this fascinating city through plans, maps and paintings.

The Golden Age is brought to life in rooms 5–12, but there is also an interesting section on 20th- and 21st-century Amsterdam, covering the Nazi occupation and efforts to protect and preserve the city. Tiny details, such as the relief above the Kalverstraat entrance, which asks people to support the upkeep of the orphanage, also point to the museum's original purpose.

Rembrandt's ruins

The old medieval Town Hall burnt down in 1652 while the building that is now Koninklijk Paleis was being built to replace it. Rembrandt provided a record of the scene when, curiously, he drew the old building in ruins, rather than the new one rising beside it.

The Dam

Once out of the museum, walk north. Take Kalverstraat or, if you find it a little too busy for comfort, take Rokin, which runs parallel to Kalverstraat to the right. This wide street was once also a canal, part of which was drained and filled in to allow better access for modern forms of transport. On the far side of the canal you will see the elegant Georgian façade of the **Allard Pierson Museum** (open Tues–Fri 10am–5pm, Sat–Sun 1–5pm; admission charge), the archaeological collection of the University of Amsterdam, which often has superb temporary exhibitions. Another couple of minutes' strolling will bring you to the **Dam**, the square that is the symbolic heart of the city.

Koninklijk Paleis

The Dam is a wide cobbled square dominated by the ornate façade of the **Koninklijk Paleis** (Royal Palace; closed for renovation until early 2008; open hours vary due to official functions; <www.koninklijkhuis.nl>; admission charge), which was completed in 1655. It was originally built as the Town Hall, facing the landing wharfs along Damrak, which at that time would have been busy with ships. The classical design by Jacob van Campen gives some indication of the confidence of the city in the Golden Age – a statue of Atlas carrying the world on his shoulders sits astride the rear of the building, and in the sumptuous interior, only the best materials were used.

When Louis Bonaparte, brother of Napoleon, became King of Holland in 1806, he demanded a palace suitable for his position and in 1808 requisitioned the Town Hall. He furnished it with the finest pieces of the time and left them all behind only two years later when he was forced out of power. It has remained a royal palace ever since, used for ceremonial occasions only.

Nieuwe Kerk, Nationaal Monument and Waxworks

Beside the palace is the **Nieuwe Kerk** (New Church; open daily 10am–6pm, Thur till 10pm when there are exhibitions, but hours may vary; free when no exhibition), built before the palace, but not the oldest church in the city, hence its name. The church has suffered several fires during its history and was stripped of all its treasures in the Alteration. The pulpit is notable for being extremely ornate for a Protestant place of worship. The church is now used as a cultural centre.

Across the Dam is the stark, white **Nationaal Monument** commemorating the role of the Dutch in World War II.

The Dam and its magnificent Koninklijk Paleis

Bicycles for hire, see page 107

On the Dam's south side stands **Madame Tussaud's** (open daily 10am–5.30pm; admission charge), a branch of the London waxworks' museum. Not only can you see celebrities modelled in wax here, but there's also a panorama recreating Amsterdam's Golden Age.

Make your way behind the Royal Palace to Raadhuisstraat, which leads to the northern canal ring (Herengracht, Keizersgracht and Prinsengracht). Immediately behind the palace is **Magna Plaza**, built in 1899 as the main post office for the city, although its Gothic architecture was considered far too ornate for a civil-service department when it was first opened. It was refurbished in 1990 and is now home to the city's premier shopping mall.

Around Raadhuisstraat

Raadhuisstraat is the main thoroughfare to the northwestern canal ring and is busy with trams, buses and cars. It will take you quickly to the main attractions of the area but it is not the prettiest or quietest route. Wandering the smaller alleys and lanes to the north and south is much more fulfilling.

Just off Raadhuisstraat, at Herengracht 168, visit the **Theatermuseum** (open Mon–Fri 11am–5pm, Sat–Sun 1–5pm; admission charge) – not only for the theatrical memorabilia, but also for the rare chance to enter a superb 17th-century residence. The grey sandstone house was built in neo-classical style by architect Philips Vingboons and sports the city's first neck gable. The museum extends into the red-brick **Bartolotti House** at Nos 170–2, an ornate Dutch Renaissance mansion built in 1617 by Hendrick de Keyser and his son Pieter. Illuminated 18th-century ceilings by Jacob de Wit grace the interior.

Westerkerk

Follow Raadhuisstraat until you reach the **Westerkerk** (open Apr–Jun and Sept Mon–Fri 11am–3pm, Jul–Aug Mon–Sat 11am–3pm; free; <www.westerkerk.nl>), set in its own square on the left and overlooking Prinsengracht. This church was designed by Hendrick de Keyser in 1619 and was one of his last commissions. It is reputed to be the burial place of Rembrandt, but no one knows the exact location of the grave (which may no longer exist). One of his pupils, Gerard de Lairesse, painted the organ panels, added in 1686.

At a café near Prinsengracht

In summer you can climb the Westerkerk's tower (Mon–Sat 10am–5pm; admission charge), the tallest in the city at 83m (273ft), offering incomparable views. The crown on top of the bell tower is a replica of the one that was presented to the city in 1489 by Maximilian I, Holy Roman Emperor.

Statue of Anne Frank

Anne Frank House

Turn left beyond the church to Prinsengracht 263, just an ordinary canal house-cum-office but made famous worldwide by what happened here in World War II. This is the **Anne Frankhuis** (Anne Frank House; open mid-Mar–mid-Sept daily 9am–9pm, mid-Sept–mid-Mar daily 9am–7pm, closed Yom Kippur; admission charge; <www.annefrank. org>), where during the Nazi occupation of Amsterdam this young girl, her family and a small group of others hid for two years in an attempt to avoid deportation.

Anne wrote a diary that paints a clear and terrifying picture of the life the family lived. It comes to an eerie stop only a few days before the family was betrayed and sent to concentration camps. Of the eight people in hiding, only Anne's father survived – Anne died of typhus only weeks before the war ended – and after the war, in 1947, he published the diary, which became a symbol for the oppression of humankind.

The house, built in 1635, has been left much as it was at the time that Anne hid here. It opened as a museum in 1960. The secret rooms upstairs, where the family spent the daylight hours, are stark and bleak. A couple of magazine pin-ups still adorn one wall. The wooden bookcase, which hid the doorway to their refuge, is still in situ, propped open for visitors to climb the few stairs to their home. Downstairs were the offices and warehouses of Mr Frank's business, which have been recreated in a multimillion-dollar development opened in 1999. Two adjacent buildings have been bought by the museum and refurbished, adding much-needed exhibition and audio-visual space, without compromising No. 263 itself. You can see videos of Anne's story and of Amsterdam under occupation, along with photographs and artefacts of the time.

The Anne Frankhuis also acts as an education centre and resource for political and philosophical groups fighting oppression in the present day. The museum is always busy in the afternoon: try to visit in the morning if possible (or in the late evening during the extended opening hours in summer).

The Jordaan

Cross Prinsengracht to reach the area of the city known as the **Jordaan**. Built as housing for workers and artisans in the early 17th century, it extends roughly from the far bank of Prinsengracht to Lijnbaansgracht and from Brouwersgracht (Brewers Canal) south to Leidseplein. Many of the streets were named after fragrant flowers but this was not the prettiest or sweetest smelling area of Amsterdam in its heyday. Overcrowding was rife and with industries such as fabric-dyeing carried out on the ground floors, it was an unsanitary place to live.

Its name is said to derive from the French word *jardin*, since a large contingent of French Huguenots came

Creativity in the Jordaan

to live here to escape from political persecution in their homeland. Today, the Jordaan has been revived and has become a fashionable residential location. You'll find many bars, restaurants and interesting boutiques in the area. It's a good place to browse for an unusual souvenir.

Rozengracht, a hectic multi-ethnic street, marks a Jordaan dividing line. The section to the north of here, and more particularly above Westerstraat, is a maze of alleys, quiet restaurants and thriving workshops, and retains many of its working-class roots. It has many true Jordaaners – traditionally, those who live close enough to the Westertoren to be able to hear the tinkling of its bells – independent-minded students, crafts and tradespeople born and bred in the quarter. The section below Rozengracht is more gentrified, with individualistic shops on lovely side streets adjacent to the larger canals, and numerous brown cafés.

Video installation at the Stedelijk Museum Bureau Amsterdam

Stedelijk Museum Bureau Amsterdam

A point of interest for fans of cutting-edge art is the **Stedelijk Museum Bureau Amsterdam** (open Tues– Sun 11am–5pm; free), at Rozenstraat 59. This off-shoot of the city's modern art museum is where the most promising, and occasionally the most peculiar, contemporary art being created in the city gets an airing. With the parent museum's Museum-plein premises closed until 2009, and the permanent collection occupying tempo-rary quarters near Centraal Station *(see page 27)*, there may be some more main-stream modern art on dis-play here for a while.

Saving the Jordaan

In the 1970s, parts of the Jordaan were earmarked for demolition, but thanks to widespread protests, the narrow streets were pre-served, complete with peri-od features such as these antique street lamps.

Amsterdamse Bos

The Netherlands suffered economic stagnation during the late 1920s and 1930s, as did the majority of other developed countries. One of the methods used to relieve the problems of unemployment was to organise large community projects that were funded by the government. One of these was the **Amsterdamse Bos** or Amsterdam Wood, which created the largest recreation area in the city. The park is on the southern fringes of the city and can be reached by one of a number of buses (Nos 170 or 172).

In 1967, it was enlarged to its present 800 hectares (2,000 acres). The trees and plants are now well established, and the wood has become an important habitat for birds, small mammals and insects, making this more than just a park. It has meadows, woodland and a huge lake for rowing, sailing and hourly rowing-boat hire. It features nature reserves, animal enclosures and a botanical garden. With around 48km (30 miles) of bicycle paths and close to 160km (100 miles) of footpaths, there is room for everybody. The stables at Amsterdamse Bos offer woodland horse rides, a perfect way to clear the city air from your system (contact Amsterdamse Manege; tel: 643 1432). There is also an open-air theatre, which holds performances in the summer.

In summer locals enjoy an activity called 'day camping', which means heading for an open space, erecting a tent and spending the day relaxing around it – perhaps with a barbecue. At the end of the day, they take the tent down and head home.

Clogs

Clogs, the native footwear of the Netherlands, are still worn by many people who find them as practical as they ever were. Clogs are traditionally made from poplar or willow – two trees that are commonly planted on the river and *polder* banks because they can soak up as much as 1,000 litres (265 gallons) of water per tree per day, keeping water levels under control. The shoes are carved from freshly felled wood and after being shaped are left to dry and harden.

Clogs are traditionally worn two sizes larger than a person's shoe size, with thick socks to fit loosely to avoid rubbing the skin. Only ceremonial clogs (and those for tourists) are painted; everyday pairs are simple and unadorned. You often see farmers and sailors wearing them. Some road workers and deliverymen also find them more comfortable than standard protective boots.

Traditional windmills at Zaanse Schans

EXCURSIONS

There are plenty of places within easy day-trip range of Amsterdam, a selection of which we cover in this chapter. Heading out of the city for a day (or two) will enable you to discover the Netherlands on a different level, whether climbing inside a windmill, walking along an historic canal that inspired the young Rembrandt, or eating pancakes in a pastoral village.

Some of the excursions covered below are served by coach tours (ask for details at the tourist office, *see pages 128–9*), though you can also find your own way by bus, train, bicycle or rented car.

Villages to the North

To the north of Amsterdam are several small towns that not only provide a contrast to the city landscape, they also take you to the heart of agricultural North Holland.

Windmills

After the invention of the first sawmill in 1592, more than 1,000 windmills were built in the Zaan region, many to provide power for sawing timber for the Zaan shipyards. Eight mills can be seen at Zaanse Schans today, and a ninth is being rebuilt.

Zaanse Schans

One such village is **Zaanse Schans**, a patch of archetypal Dutch landscape just a few kilometres north of Amsterdam centre, near the town of Zaandam. This landscape is no accident or happy coincidence but a living museum created in 1960, which has brought together a number of farmhouses, windmills, dairies and barns – real agricultural buildings that would have been demolished had they not been relocated here. Zaanse Schans has working mills, cheese-making factories and a clog workshop, situated on a canalside. You are free to explore at your own pace and maybe enjoy a *pannekoek* (pancake) while you're there.

Broek in Waterland and Monnickendam

Broek in Waterland is a village situated just north of the city environs. A small collection of quaint wooden houses, it is surrounded by canals and streams.

Further north is **Monnickendam**, once a large fishing port on the Zuiderzee which lost its *raison d'être* when the Afsluitdijk was completed in 1932, creating the freshwater lake called the IJsselmeer. The pretty gabled buildings that line the main street were once cottages for fisherfolk, and the small port still plays host to a fleet of ships. Many are now in private hands, or work as pleasure boats in the summer season. There is also a large, private marina filled with sailing boats which head out on to the open water on any sunny weekend. Walk around the old port to find vestiges of the traditional lifestyle. A few families still fish for eels and process them in small 'factories' along the quayside (although most 'IJsselmeer' eels are are now imported). In summer you can buy them from stalls in the town. There are also some good fish restaurants around the harbour.

Marken

Just 5km (3 miles) beyond Monnickendam is **Marken**, one of the most beautiful villages in the Netherlands and home to a community of Calvinist Dutch whose traditions reach back hundreds of years. Situated on an island, Marken had no vehicle access until 1957, when a causeway was opened, linking the village to the mainland. Today the community welcomes visitors but not their cars, which must be left in a large car park on the outskirts.

A few of the older inhabitants of this close-knit community still wear traditional Dutch costume as everyday wear.

Traditional boats moored in Monnickendam

Volendam village on the IJsselmeer

You can walk through the village with its traditional painted wooden houses to the picture-perfect harbour. Stop at the tiny museum on the quayside, which holds an eclectic mix of seafaring and fishing memorabilia.

Between Monnickendam and Marken, the causeway leads out into open water that is home to thousands of birds in the summer. The native herons, ducks and moorhens see many species of migratory birds that fly north for the summer and return south as the winter approaches. The road is also very good for cycling, being flat and smooth, and for walking. Head out towards the old lighthouse at the far end of Marken island, which stands on a lonely promontory.

Volendam and Edam

North of Marken and Monnickendam is **Volendam**, a Catholic counterpart to the Protestant Marken. It is perhaps the village most changed by tourism, with cafés and souvenir shops lining the harbour. Volendam is still noted for its fish (there are several good restaurants and herring stands along the harbour) and for its distinctive local dress, especially the winged lace caps worn by women.

The town of **Edam**, famed for its red- or yellow-rinded cheese, has a pretty **Kaaswaag** (Cheese Weigh House) dating from 1592. Look out for the wonderfully named **Kwakelbrug** – the narrowest old bridge in town, wide enough only for single-file foot traffic. The centre of town has an unusual paved overlock, the **Damsluis**, just below the **Captain's House**, dating from 1540. Despite its world renown, Edam is still unspoiled and there are some pretty restaurants where you can enjoy lunch before heading back to the city.

Haarlem

Haarlem, situated only 19km (12 miles) west of Amsterdam, was the home of Antwerp-born Frans Hals, father of the Dutch School of painting. The centre of town is a maze of narrow streets filled with historic buildings, all of which fall under the shadow of the 15th-century **Sint-Bavokerk** (St

Sint-Bavokerk, Haarlem

Bavo's Church; open Mon–Sat 10am–4pm; admission charge), an enormous Gothic edifice which contains one of the finest organs in Europe, installed in 1735. Handel and Mozart both played the instrument, and you can hear it for yourself on Tuesday evenings and Thursday afternoons in summer when free recitals fill the church with music.

Across Lepelstraat from the church is the **Vleeshal** (meat market) from 1603. The **Frans Hals Museum** (open Tues–Sat 11am–5pm, Sun and holidays noon–5pm; admission charge; <www.franshalsmuseum.com>), on Groot Heiligland to the south, is a suitable testimony to the town's most famous son, who was still painting in his eighties. The museum was opened in 1913 at the site of an old men's home.

On the banks of the River Spaarne is the **Teylers Museum** (open Tues–Sat 10am–5pm, Sun and holidays noon–5pm; admission charge), founded by silk merchant Pieter Teyler van der Hulst in 1778 and said to be the Netherlands' oldest public collection. Teyler, having no heir, bequeathed his fortune to the advancement of the arts and sciences, and there is an interesting collection of scientific instruments among other artefacts. The museum has collections ranging from minerals and fossils to medals and coins.

Frans Hals Museum

Floral Glory

Every spring, from early April to the end of May, the fields south of Haarlem and Amsterdam erupt in a rainbow of colour, which stretches as far as the eye can see. The Dutch tulips attract thousands of visitors for these few weeks of beauty.

Another attraction for flower lovers, near the town of Lisse, is **Keukenhof**, a 28-hectare (69-acre) showpiece flower garden that welcomes the public (open late Mar–late May daily 8am–7.30pm; admission charge; <www.keukenhof.nl>). You'll find a host of spectacular crocus, hyacinth and narcissus blooms along with the tulips. The landscape at Keukenhof is planted with stately beech and oak trees, enhanced by pretty windmills which add to the authentic Dutch feel. There is also a restaurant and gift shop where you can buy bulbs, blooms and souvenirs.

Flowers in Keukenhof

In **Aalsmeer** you can visit the vast **Bloemenveiling** or flower auction hall at Legmeerdijk (open Mon–Fri 7.30–11am; admission charge). Every day (get there as early as possible) millions of blooms are auctioned, which are then dispatched around the world within hours. It's fascinating to watch the action, as miniature trains carry the flowers through the auction hall for the buyers to assess, and a large electronic bid-taker on the wall reflects the current bidding price. The sheer size of the auction house is what gives pause for thought – the walkway for spectators is 1.6km (1 mile) long.

Leiden

The rich history and university atmosphere makes Leiden an interesting place to visit. Just a half-hour by train from Amsterdam, this medieval city, famous for its cloth-making and brewing industries, joined the Dutch Revolt against Spain and was besieged. It eventually rallied after the dykes were broken and the land was flooded, enabling a rescue fleet to sail directly across the countryside and save the city.

Rembrandt was born in Leiden, as were other Dutch Masters such as Gerrit Dou, Jan Steen, Gabriel Metsu and Jan van Gooyen. This is also where the Pilgrim Fathers formed a community in 1608, seeking refuge from persecution in

England. Leiden University is probably the most prestigious in the Netherlands, with alumni including René Descartes and the 17th-century lawyer, Hugo Grotius.

Visit the **De Valk** windmill on Tweede Binnenvestgracht, which is now a museum, and the **Stedelijk Museum De Lakenhal** on Oude Singel, with its rooms illuminating Leiden's history. The inner city is ringed by two concentric canals, so a stretch of water is never far away, and there are many bridges to cross. Make your way to the marketplace where the old and new branches of the Rhine meet and open markets are held on Wednesday and Saturday. Then cross the bridge to Oude Rijn and turn right towards the **Burcht**, Leiden's 12th-century castle. Have a drink at the Koetshuis in the courtyard. The **Botanical Gardens** along Wittesingel are also worth a visit.

Alkmaar

Dutch cheeses are world renowned, and the small red and yellow Edam and Gouda rounds can be found in supermarkets and grocery stores in just about every country of the Western world. However, in the Netherlands, cheese isn't so much an industry as a way of life, and tradition still has a part to play in the production and distribution of the product.

Make love not war

Alkmaar's municipal museum, Stedelijk Museum Alkmaar, is housed in an attractive Renaissance guild house. It contains the notable 16th-century Siege of Alkmaar; bizarrely, the painting shows a couple making love while the battle rages.

Alkmaar is a small town 30km (19 miles) north of Amsterdam. It has been the centre of cheese production for many centuries and is now the only town that still has a market dedicated to cheese, held every Friday morning during the summer. There's also another busy market in town on Friday, for produce other than cheese.

Alkmaar cheese porters

The 14th-century **Waaggebouw** was a chapel before being converted into a weigh house. On Fridays the square in front of it becomes a showcase of cheese. Rounds of cheese are piled there waiting to be weighed. Porters, dressed in white trousers, white top and coloured hat, transport them on wooden sleds with shoulder harnesses and playfully attempt to be the fastest, much to the amusement of the crowds.

The Waaggebouw contains the **Hollands Kaasmuseum** (Holland Cheese Museum; open Apr–Oct Mon–Thur and Sat 10am–4pm, Fri 9am–4pm, Christmas and New Year 10am–4pm, hours vary for other public holidays; admission charge).

Nearby, the **Grote Kerk** (Large Church; open Tues–Sun 10am–5pm; admission charge) contains the tomb of the count of Holland Floris V, who granted Amsterdam its rights to carry goods toll-free in the 13th century. In a sense he started the economic life of the city and could be said to be its founding father.

WHAT TO DO

SHOPPING

Amsterdam is a gold mine for those who like to browse. The city has not yet been taken over by the international chain stores, and the narrow streets of the centre, the canal rings and the Jordaan area are home to myriad small, independent boutiques, where you can wander for hours in search of that individual gift. The nearest Amsterdam has to 'international' shopping is Kalverstraat, a street that's home to trendy, if mostly undistinguished, fashion outlets and department stores, and P.C. Hooftstraat, noted for its designer names.

Most museums have good gift shops, especially the Jewish Historical Museum, Maritime Museum, Amsterdam Historical Museum, NEMO and the Nieuwe Kerk. The Rijksmuseum and Van Gogh Museum have a shared shop on Museumplein.

Amsterdammers love to shop for their homes. Although many live in small apartments, what they lack in floor space they make up for in the quality of their environments, and interior design stores feature in every shopping area.

Markets

Amsterdam still has a good number of authentic street markets where you can mix with locals and pick up a bargain. Some markets cater to those with a specialist interest and are by no means a place where you'll always find inferior or cheap goods. Perhaps the most famous market is the **Bloemenmarkt** (Flower Market), which is held on the Singel every day. As well as beautiful blooms you can buy bulbs and tubers to take home (if your country's customs authorities allow this).

Colourful clogs

The **flea market on Waterlooplein** also has an international reputation, although the market is much smaller since the building of the Muziektheater. Many stallholders have moved to other locations in the city, although second-hand clothes still feature heavily, along with ethnic wear. It is open every day except Sunday.

On Elandsgracht and Looiersgracht in the Jordaan is a market for cheaper antiques, collectables and bric-a-brac. The stalls are found inside a number of old houses, which makes it the perfect place to shop on a rainy day.

There is a **Boekenmarkt** (Book Market) every Friday on Spui in front of the private entrance to the Begijnhof. Publications in various languages are on sale.

The **Kunstmarkt** (Art Market) on Thorbeckeplein takes place on Sundays between March and November. This is a forum for independent artists in all genres.

A summer **Antiekmarkt** (Antiques Market) meets at Nieuwmarkt on Sundays from May to October.

The **Postzegelmarkt** (Stamp Market) on Nieuwezijds Voorburgwal attracts collectors on Wednesday and Saturday afternoons, while the **Albert Cuypmarkt**, selling everything

The Nine Little Streets

The Negen Straatjes (Nine Little Streets) are a number of small alleys that form the ribs linking the Herengracht, Keizersgracht and Prinsengracht canals. Here you will find some very individual boutiques with imports from all over the world, as well as antiques shops and designer clothing shops. It's also a great place for small restaurants and bars.

For designer fashions, visit P.C. Hooftstraat and Van Baerlestraat, which border Museumplein. Although this couture quarter is small compared with that of Milan or Paris, you'll still find a good range to choose from, and stores stock work by international and Dutch designers.

Inside De Looier, an antiques market in the Jordaan

from fruit and vegetables to textiles from Monday to Saturday, is one of the largest general street markets in Europe.

What to Buy

Antiques. The rich legacy of the Dutch colonial period makes Amsterdam one of the most interesting cities for antiques. European period furniture mixes with Southeast Asian artefacts and art – there are dealers in almost every different specialist area. This is not a place for amateur collectors. Prices are high but so is quality, the expertise of the dealers, and the advice that they give. Many of the finest shops are found around Nieuwe Spiegelstraat and the small streets leading from the Rijksmuseum back towards the city centre, and there are also a number on Rokin.

If you prefer the antiques of tomorrow there are also many stores selling 'collectables'. Most popular are early 20th-century light fittings, taps and door furniture. The VVV

Gay kitsch for sale in the
Red Light District

(see page 129–30) produces a leaflet entitled *Spiegel-kwartier: Arts and Antiques in Amsterdam* with a list of the city's specialist dealers and their details.

Art. The lure of the city for creative people has existed for centuries and modern artists follow in the wake of Rembrandt and the Dutch Masters. Dozens of small galleries offer everything from classical to pop art. Exhibitions at the major galleries also promote the work of up-and-coming younger artists as well as established names. Street art is also very much in evidence, especially in the summer. For those who enjoy a more classic form of art, paintings and prints of windmills or canal houses can be found all across the city.

Diamonds. Before World War II, Amsterdam was a major centre for the buying and polishing of diamonds. The industry was decimated by the loss of many Jewish families who ran the major diamond houses, but a slow recovery ensured its survival. Today the industry is known for the quality of its polishing and the expertise of its independent traders.

Five main diamond houses in the city are responsible for buying and polishing the majority of the stones. They sell to smaller dealers but also to the public. You'll be able to see diamond polishers at work before you buy. You can choose from loose stones or finished pieces of jewellery. The five are: Amsterdam Diamond Centre on Rokin (corner Dam); Coster Diamonds on Paulus Potterstraat facing Museumplein; Gassan Diamonds on Nieuwe Uilenburgerstraat; Van Moppes on Albert Cuypstraat; and Stoeltie Diamonds on Wagenstraat.

Plants. The Netherlands is famed worldwide for its flowers, and particularly the beautiful spring tulip displays in the fields to the west and southwest of Amsterdam. Yet blooms are produced all year in hothouses scattered across the countryside and can be purchased at the Bloemenmarkt on the Singel. In addition to fresh flowers you can also buy bulbs to take home. The streets of Amsterdam have many independent florists with imaginative ideas in fresh and dried flowers. Even if you don't buy, it may well inspire you for your return home.

Cigars. There is a small but high-quality cigar industry in the Netherlands offering a wide choice in terms of size and price. P.G.C. Hajenius on Rokin have been producing their own brand and importing the best in the world for 170 years. They also have a smoking café if you want to sit and enjoy your cigar on the premises. Their shop, specially built for the

Bulbs to buy at the Bloemenmarkt

Blue and white Delftware

company in 1915, has a beautiful Art Deco interior.

Jenever. Only the Dutch and Belgians produce this alcoholic drink, a kind of hybrid of English gin and German *schnapps*. It is often bottled in distinctive stone flagons, which make wonderful souvenirs – and excellent rustic candlesticks when empty (as you can see in the city's many 'brown bars').

Pewter. You'll find old pewter objects in the Amsterdam Historical Museum and the Scheepvaartmuseum. In the Golden Age, pewter was used to make everyday utensils such as mugs, plates and kettles. Today, it is fashioned into all kinds of objects, although larger pieces are expensive.

Silver. Modern silver is fashioned into a range of objects and styles of jewellery. You'll also find lots of older pieces – some quite exquisite – in shops around the town in the form of spoons, ornate pill and snuff boxes, or letter openers.

Delftware. The pottery style known as Delft (after the city southwest of Amsterdam) was produced across the country during the Golden Age and, in the 1600s, many fine pieces came out of a pottery on Prinsengracht. The blue and white finish is standard Delft, and you will find it at many high-class outlets with prices to match the quality. For an eclectic selection of old and new Delftware, visit Galleria d'Arte Rinascimento, Prinsengracht 170. At Delftshop, with branches at Prinsengracht 440, Rokin 44, Muntplein 12 and Spiegelgracht 13, you can buy examples of the traditional pottery styles, and some fine modern pieces too.

Other Dutch souvenirs. You'll find a range of souvenirs that epitomise the Holland of tourist brochures. Wooden clogs feature prominently, either plain or painted in bright colours. Windmills are found everywhere, on tea-towels, T-shirts or fridge magnets.

ENTERTAINMENT

It is said that there are over 40 different performances taking place every evening of the year in Amsterdam, so you will not be at a loss for things to do. Concert halls and theatres are found all across the city with ballet, opera, rock, jazz and classical performances all featured regularly. There are also plenty of venues for more risqué or avant-garde performances.

Late-night jazz

The main venues for major performances are the Concertgebouw near to Museumplein (for orchestral and chamber concerts); the Muziektheater (on the banks of the Amstel), which is home to the National Ballet and the Netherlands Opera; and Beurs van Berlage, the beautiful old Stock Exchange building near the Dam, now a twin-hall concert venue and home to the Netherlands Philharmonic Orchestra and the Netherlands Chamber Orchestra.

The neon lights of Damrak

The city's newest large musical venue is the Muziekgebouw aan 't IJ, on the south bank of the IJ waterway, just east of Centraal Station. It houses the former De IJsbreker modern and experimental music centre and, in an annexe, the renowned Bimhuis jazz and blues club.

The Koninklijk Theater Carré, near the Magere Brug on the Amstel, hosts musicals. Boom Chicago in Leidseplein is the venue for stand-up comedy in English. Melkweg on Lijnbaansgracht is an offbeat arts centre-cum-club, with concert hall, disco, experimental plays (some in English) and art exhibitions.

You can book tickets for performances on arrival but popular acts sell out quickly, so reserve in advance if there is something you particularly wish to see. The easiest way to book tickets in advance is through the Amsterdam Uit Bureau (AUB-Uitlijn). They produce a monthly magazine called *Uitkrant* with a listing of major performances (in Dutch, but listings are fairly easy to follow). Contact them on tel: 0900 0191 (have your credit card ready). Tickets can either be posted to your home address or kept at the AUB office in Leidseplein for you to collect at a later date. When in Amsterdam, pick up their English brochure, *Culture in Amsterdam*, at the AUB's office.

At any given time there will be temporary art exhibitions at galleries and museums around the city. The Nederlands Filmmuseum in Vondelpark (due to move to Amsterdam North in 2009) also holds special showings and film festivals.

The Holland Festival is a programme of art events that take place across the country throughout June. In

Day by Day

The monthly magazine *Amsterdam Day by Day*, published by the VVV, lists the performances and exhibitions taking place each day throughout the city.

Amsterdam, parks and squares are filled with organised activities, and many galleries and concert halls hold events. A ticket line provides information about the activities and tickets if you pay by credit card (tel: 788 2100).

The Holland Casino Amsterdam at Max Euweplein off Leidseplein (open every day from 1.30pm) offers the opportunity for adults to try their luck (tel: 521 1111).

There is no shortage of discos and nightclubs, particularly in the streets around Leidseplein and Rembrandtplein – those in favour change by the month, so just follow the crowds if you want to find the most 'happening' venue.

Cruising the canals in a tour boat is an excellent way of viewing the city. Many of the bridges and historic buildings are lit at night, and it is possible to cruise the canals while eating dinner. The Rederij Lovers company *(see page 117)* offers wine and cheese cruises or full dinner cruises. For a more private cruise (on which you can arrange your own itinerary) you can hire a water taxi.

SPORTS

Football

This is an incredibly popular sport in the Netherlands, and Ajax, the Amsterdam team, has been one of the most successful in Europe for more than 30 years. Ajax play at the Amsterdam ArenA, a fine modern stadium used for numerous sporting events. It is almost impossible to obtain tickets in Amsterdam, but you can buy a travel package that includes match tickets from the Ajax website <www.ajax.nl>.

Watersports

With so much water around the city, it's not surprising that water-based sports are very popular. Even on the city-centre canals you'll find pedalos (sometimes called water cycles) to hire, so you can explore the sights under your own steam. Contact Canal Bike on 626 5574. You can also captain your own boat to explore the area. Canal Motorboats has a dock at the Zandhoek marina on Realen Island, which is west of Centraal Station (tel: 422 7007 for information and reservations).

On the wider waterways outside the old part of town you will find rowing and sailing clubs that take to the open water in good weather all year round. Out on the IJsselmeer (the freshwater lake that was the Zuiderzee) on any sunny weekend you'll see hundreds of white and brown sails breaking the horizon. Boats can be hired for trips out on the water from Monnickendam or you can take a trip on a crewed boat, although you'll need to make a booking well in advance. Contact Holland Zeilcharters Monnickendam at 't Prooyen 4a, 1141 VD Monnickendam; tel: 0299 652351; <www.sailing.nl>.

Cycling

Although the Dutch spend more time than most people riding bikes as commuters, cycling for fun is also one of the major recreational activities. Cycle routes run parallel to most roadways, making longer journeys relatively easy, and sporting groups or families will head out to villages such as Monnickendam or Marken. Closer to the centre, a ride through Vondelpark gives you a feeling of being out of the city. If you would like to tour with a group, contact Yellow

Bike Guided Tours, Nieuwezijds Kolk 29; tel: 620 6940; they organise daily tours with English guides between April and October. *(For bike hire, see page 107.)*

Skating

Winter sports have traditionally played a big part in the lives of Amsterdammers and people from North Holland. When the rivers and canals freeze in winter, everyone is out skating – with long-distance skating through the countryside from town to town on cold, bright Sundays.

CHILDREN

Amsterdam has many attractions and activities to keep younger visitors occupied, and those mentioned overleaf *(detailed in the Where to Go section)* offer only a selection.

Cycling with the kids in tow, Amsterdam-style

The distinctive shape of the NEMO Science Centre

Try the science centre at **NEMO**, where experiments with energy, looking at cells in the human body through a microscope, or playing some virtual reality games will inspire most children *(see page 49)*. The enduringly popular waxworks of **Madame Tussaud's** present all the latest stars of music and films, so that the kids can try to guess who the figures are before reading the exhibit details. At the **Artis** complex there is the chance to explore the zoo, aquarium and planetarium. If looking at the solar system doesn't excite your child then getting close to tigers and elephants might.

The re-creation of the Dutch trading ship at the **Scheepvaartmuseum**, with its staff playing the part of sailors, brings out the sense of adventure in children. The Children's Museum at the **Tropenmuseum** is also popular. Smaller children will enjoy the **TunFun activity centre**, beneath the busy traffic junction at Mr Visserplein.

Children usually love **tram rides**, which they regard as a quirky new mode of transport. And be sure to take them on a **canal cruise** – seeing a city from a different perspective is great fun and a good education.

If you visit Amsterdam in early December children will enjoy the parade as Sinterklaas (St Nicholas) visits the city on 5 December. He parades through the streets on horseback, before delivering gifts.

Throughout the summer there are activities in the major parks and squares. Street theatre, face-painting and hands-on art shows will ignite the kids' enthusiasm and interest.

Calendar of Events

25 February Commemoration of the 'February Strike' led by the dockers against the Nazis in 1941, held on Jonas Daniël Meijerplein.

15 March (closest Sunday) Stille Omgang – a silent procession through the city to commemorate the 14th-century 'Miracle' of the Host.

Late March Opening of Keukenhof Gardens, 30km (19 miles) south-west of Amsterdam.

30 April Koninginnedag, the Queen's official birthday. Street markets, street parties, fireworks and festivities throughout the city.

4 May Dodenherdenking: National Remembrance Day.

5 May Bevrijdingsdag (Liberation Day): a smaller version of Queen's Day *(see above)*, held mostly in Vondelpark.

June Holland Festival at the Stadsschouwburg and other venues, featuring theatrical, operatic, dance and musical events. Open Gardens Days (three days in the middle of June): gardens of canal houses and museums along Herengracht, Keizersgracht and Prinsengracht open to visitors.

July Over Het IJ Festival: the old NDSM Wharf on the north side of the IJ waterway is the focus for 10 days of modern theatre, music and dance.

July–September Free concerts and theatre afternoons and evening in the open-air pavilion in Vondelpark.

Early August Gay Pride: exuberant festival culminating in a colourful boat parade on Prinsengracht.

August Grachten Festival: a five-day mid-month feast of classical music, with concerts held at venues along the canals. The highlight is the Prinsengracht Concert, on a pontoon moored outside the Pulitzer Hotel.

Last week in August Uitmarkt, a week of free music, dance and theatre performances at major squares around the city.

Mid-November Sinterklaas arrives from Spain and travels through the streets of Amsterdam.

5 December Sinterklaas's saint's day and *Pakjesavond* or Parcels Evening, when he delivers his gifts to the children.

31 December New Year's Eve fireworks around Amsterdam harbour and the Nieuwmarkt/Chinatown area.

EATING OUT

Dutch national cuisine has a limited range of dishes, yet eating out in Amsterdam can be one of the highlights of the trip. The reason? Many of the more than 100 nationalities that inhabit the city have brought their own unique culinary delights to Amsterdam's restaurants. You could stay in the city for over a month and not eat the same style of food twice. This offers boundless opportunities to try something new, and means you'll never get tired of eating out.

Amsterdam is a café society, and restaurants and bars form a lively part of the social scene. Restaurants range from the very formal to the informal, with prices to match.

Brown Cafés

Amsterdam's traditional brown cafés (so-called because walls and ceilings have turned brown from age and smoke) are identified by dark, cosy, wooden interiors. The only audible sound is the buzz of lively conversation and the tinkle of glasses being rinsed. Coffee is generally brewed, not machine-made, and if you fancy a snack to go with your beer or spirit, there is usually a plate of olives or cheese. These cafés define the Dutch word *gezelligheid*, which means a state of cosiness or conviviality. This is where locals come for a few beers after work, to play cards, engage in political debates and tell tall tales.

The more elegant and stylish grand cafés in the city serve lunch and desserts, and tend to have high ceilings, more light, reading tables and a wider variety of music than brown cafés. There are also cafés where you can play chess, throw darts, or play pool or billiards. There are men's cafés, women's cafés and even night cafés, which close around 5am.

Dutch Dishes

Traditional Dutch food is seasonal and based on whatever was harvested from the land or the sea, with light summer dishes and hearty, filling winter foods. Arable farms abound in the countryside, and meat dishes do not generally play a major part in Dutch cuisine. Fish and dairy produce are always considerably more prevalent.

Daily specials

The Dutch breakfast *(ontbijt)* is a hearty one. Slices of ham and cheese, and perhaps boiled eggs with various breads and jam or honey are accompanied by strong milky coffee.

For lunch the Dutch enjoy *pannekoeken*, pancakes thicker than the French *crêpe* and made fresh as you order them. You can have savoury ones (made with eggs and bacon, for instance) or sweet toppings, with fruit, chocolate and cream, or perhaps even one of each. *Uitsmijter* is another interesting and popular lunch dish, served in Dutch homes and in cafés. It consists of a slice of bread toasted on one side on to which a slice of ham and a fried egg are added.

Broodjes or sandwiches are popularly available with a vast range of fillings. The local ham and Dutch cheeses are probably the most authentic if you want to eat local, and the combination is delicious eaten hot in a *toastje* or toasted sandwich.

Patates frites (chips, French fries) are served and eaten at any time of day – you'll see the vendors' stalls in squares or on street corners. They are thickly cut and served with a spoonful of deliciously thick mayonnaise.

Smoked eels

Winter dishes are warming and hearty. Start with a bowl of *erwtensoep*, a thick pea soup with chunks of sausage. Served with heavy bread or pumpernickel, it constitutes a meal in itself. The other main type of soup is *bruine bonen soep* made with red kidney beans. This may then be followed by *stamppot*, a purée of potatoes and vegetables (usually kale or cabbage) served with slices of *rookworst* (thick smoked sausage), or *hutspot*, made with beef.

Fish

Fish has been a mainstay of the Dutch diet for many generations. Try halibut *(heilbot)*, cod *(kabeljauw)* or haddock *(schelvis)*, all of which come from the North Sea off the Dutch coast. Local oysters and mussels are especially good, and smoked eel is a Dutch delicacy. A dish that harks back to the Calvinists, and which is light on the palate, is a basic meal of plaice with vegetables, where the fish is grilled and served with butter. You'll also find freshwater fish, called 'sweetwater fish' by the Dutch, from some canals and rivers.

Another Dutch favourite is herring, a small Atlantic fish that swims close to the shores of the North Sea and is still caught in vast numbers. It is eaten cleaned and raw (you'll see them sold like this at stalls in the street). The typical way to eat herring is to take the tail in one hand, hold it above your mouth and slowly eat it in bites, so that the herring gradually disappears and only the tail is left. Amsterdammers often prefer their herrings chopped and served with equally raw chopped onions.

Cheese

Cheese is eaten more often at breakfast or lunch rather than with dinner. Several types of cheese from the Netherlands have become internationally famous. Both Gouda and Edam, named after the towns where they are produced, are easily identifiable, being round in shape and covered in a red (for export) or yellow wax that keeps the cheese airtight, allowing them to be kept for many months. Traditionally, they were stored in a cool larder and a large cheese could last a family several weeks.

Desserts

The Dutch aren't known for their sweet tooth, although most cafés and restaurants will have *appelgebaak* (apple pie) on the menu. You will also find *stroopwafels*, two thin, round waffles filled with golden syrup and butter; and *poffertjes*, small, shell-shaped pieces of dough, fried until brown in butter and sugar.

Cheese is eaten for breakfast or lunch in the Netherlands

Savoury and sweet pancakes

Indonesian Cuisine

The expansion of Dutch interests in the Golden Age brought a wealth of new ingredients and flavourings from the Far East. This added interest to native dishes, such as the Dutch habit of sprinkling nutmeg on cooked vegetables, but also, over the centuries, the close ties with the lands of what is now Indonesia have created a second Dutch national dish – *rijsttafel* (literally translated as 'rice table'). There are many Indonesian restaurants throughout the city offering *rijsttafel* with 10, 15 or 20 dishes.

Rijsttafel is a Dutch invention, an interpretation of Indonesian cuisine – though often less spicy than the real thing – which became accepted both in the old colonies and in the Netherlands as a meal in itself. It consists of a number of small spicy meat, fish or vegetable dishes – up to 32 in total – and a communal serving of rice. Take a serving of rice and put it in the middle of your plate, then take small amounts of the spicy dishes and place them around the outside of the rice. The small courses balance one another in taste, texture and heat (spiciness) to excite the palate.

The standard dishes include *babi* (pork), *daging bronkos* (roast meat in coconut milk), *goreng kering* (pimento and fish paste) and small skewers of meat *(satay)* with peanut sauce. Any dish that is labelled *sambal* is guaranteed to be hot (spicy), but hot dishes will be tempered with cooling dishes such as marinated fruits and vegetables. If you don't want a full *rijsttafel* try ordering *nasi rames*, a smaller selection of dishes with rice – an ideal choice for lunch.

Food of the World

Wander along just a few of Amsterdam's streets and it will soon become apparent that choice is the name of the game when it comes to eating out. If you want the best in French cuisine – and there are a number of restaurants with Michelin stars here – you will not be disappointed. Japanese restaurants abound for the very best in *sushi* or *teppanyaki*. Even good old steak can be found in Argentine, American and Mexican style.

Other European cuisines on offer are Spanish tapas bars and Greek tavernas – and you need look only a little further afield to find Egyptian kitchens, Moroccan *couscous* houses and South African bistros. All these are in addition to a fine selection of Italian and Chinese restaurants. Your trip to Amsterdam could well prove to be a culinary journey right around the world.

Indonesian cuisine at Tempo Doeloe

What to Drink

The Dutch love their bars. You'll find one on almost every street corner and they are warm, welcoming places where you can sit for hours, people-watch and, when necessary, wait for it to stop raining. The staple place to socialise is the *bruine kroeg* (brown bar), as much an institution as the pub is in Britain. So called because of their brown-stained walls, low lighting and smoky interiors, brown bars sell alcohol, coffee and light snacks. They will also have a range of newspapers and magazines for you to read (generally at least one in English) while you have your drink – it helps to promote the political and social discussions that Amsterdammers enjoy so much.

Each bar has its own character, which is essentially based around the personality of the owner and the clientele. You'll soon find one that suits you, whether your taste is for a background of dusky jazz vocals, a blast of heavy rock, or no extraneous noise at all. Bars generally open late morning or mid-afternoon and don't close until 1 or 2am. Often, if there are customers and a good atmosphere, a bar will stay open until the last person leaves.

The Coffee Shop Scene

In Amsterdam, so-called 'coffee shops' have sold cannabis under a quasi-legal status for more than 30 years. Their presence is tolerated largely because they segregate the users of soft drugs from the dealers who peddle harder substances.

There are around 300 establishments in the city where customers are able to sit back and indulge without suffering the paranoia of the wrong-doer. Ranging from unassuming neighbourhood joints to multi-level coffee shops with internet access, pool tables and TV screens, they are generally easy to spot, often having psychedelic paint schemes or depictions of the marijuana leaf on the outside.

Traditional Dutch bars have historically centered on two products. Beer is one and *jenever* (pronounced 'yen-eyfer') the other. At one time, distillers and brewers had tasting houses or *proeflokalen* for their products where buyers would convene to test the latest brews or compare vintages. Today, there are only a few of these remaining in the city and they always serve a range of other drinks, in addition to their traditional one.

Traditional brown café

De Drie Fleschjes (the Three Bottles) on Gravenstraat (behind Nieuwe Kerk) is the major *jenever* tasting house in the city, and it has changed little in appearance since it was opened in 1650 – although the distillery it used to belong to was converted into a hotel in the 1980s. Here you will be able to try different types of *jenever*. The young *(jonge)* clear *jenever* can be rather harsh to the palate, while the old *(oude)*, aged in wooden casks, which impart a slightly yellow colour, is more mellow. There are also varieties of fruit-flavoured *jenever* to try.

In de Wildeman on Kolksteeg is a tasting house for beers, and its minimalist wood-panelled rooms impart something of the feeling of a religious experience to this drink, which has been so much a part of Amsterdam life since the 13th century. There are more than 50 types of beer available on draught, supplemented by nearly 100 different beers in bottles. You'll be able to undertake a beer tour of Europe if you have the stamina.

Double Dutch cheer

Dutch-produced beer is generally a pils variety, slightly stronger than British lager or American beer. If you order beer by the glass it will usually come in a 33cl (12 fl oz) measure, served chilled. The two fingers of froth that crown your beer are traditional; they are levelled with the top of the glass with a white plastic spatula.

As well as beer and *jenever*, most bars also serve wine, coffee and soft drinks. Coffee is the lifeblood of Amsterdam. The strong black short serving of fresh brew – and it must be fresh – is sold in cafés and bars all across the city. It always comes with a sweet biscuit. Do specify when you order if you want it with milk or cream *(met melk* or *met room)*. This will arrive in a separate container.

To Help You Order…

Could we have a table?   **Heeft u een tafel voor ons?**
I'd like a/an/some…   **Ik zou graag… willen hebben**

aperitif	**een aperitief**	milk	**melk**
beer	**een bier**	mustard	**mosterd**
bread	**brood**	pepper	**peper**
butter	**boter**	potatoes	**aardappels**
coffee	**koffie**	rice	**rijst**
dessert	**een nagerecht**	salad	**sla**
fish	**vis**	salt	**zout**
fruit	**fruit**	sandwich	**een boterham**
meat	**vlees**	sugar	**suiker**
mineral water	**mineraalwater**	wine	**wijn**

... And Read The Menu

aardbeien	strawberries	**kool**	cabbage
ananas	pineapple	**lamsvlees**	lamb
biefstuk	steak	**patates frites**	French fries
bloemkool	cauliflower	**perzik**	peach
citroen	lemon	**pruimen**	plums
ei(eren)	egg(s)	**rundvlees**	beef
forel	trout	**sinaasappel**	orange
frambozen	raspberries	**uien**	onions
gehaktbal	meatball	**uitsmijter**	lunch snack of
kaas	cheese		bread, ham and
karbonade	chop		fried eggs
kersen	cherries	**varkensvlees**	pork
kip	chicken	**verse paling**	fresh eel
kokosnoot	coconut	**vrucht**	fruit
konijn	rabbit	**worstje**	sausage

In a brown bar

HANDY TRAVEL TIPS

An A–Z Summary of Practical Information

A

ACCOMMODATION *(see also* CAMPING, YOUTH HOSTELS *and the list of* RECOMMENDED HOTELS *starting on page 131)*

Amsterdam has a wide range of accommodation of all standards and price ranges, and lodging is found in most areas of the city. Hotels are rated by stars from one to five with five being the top class. Most hotels have rooms for single travellers, which are usually at 20–30 percent below the price for a double room. Prices are higher in the summer months and lower in winter. Service charge will be included in the rates but the 5 percent city tourist tax might not be, so it is worth checking.

Modern five-star hotels in the city have every convenience, although breakfast may not be included in the price. In the lower-class hotels breakfast is usually included.

Given the architectural style of the buildings in Amsterdam you will find many of the lower-class hotels have steep and narrow staircases leading to the upper floors and no lift. So check before booking, if you have problems climbing stairs or have young children. Also many of the old houses converted into hotels have rooms of varying sizes and hence varying prices, so check this as well.

The Netherlands Board of Tourism & Conventions (NBTC) offices in the UK, US, Canada and some other countries *(see pages 128–9)* will be able to provide a list of hotels in each class and price bracket. Amsterdam's VVV tourist offices *(see page 129)* can also book accommodation for you if you arrive without a reservation. This is not advisable during the summer or other school holidays (exact dates change each year but generally the the end of May and the end of October, as well as Easter and Christmas). You can book directly with a hotel or through the Netherlands Reservation Centre (NRC), Plantsoengracht 2, 1441 DE Purmerend, Netherlands; tel: (0299) 689 144; fax: (0299) 689 154; e-mail: <info@hotelres. nl>; <www.hotelres.nl> (office hours: 8.30am–5.30pm).

The VVV also offers 'arrangement packages' in alliance with various hotels. These comprise a package of accommodation with discount vouchers.

Boarding houses and B&B rooms are also available, although these will not usually have rooms with private facilities.

If you would like to live as the Amsterdammers do while on your trip, Amsterdam House acts as an agent for a number of apartments and houseboats that can be rented short or long term. They can be contacted at 's-Gravelandseveer 7, 1011 KN AE Amsterdam; tel: 626 2577; fax: 626 2987; <www.amsterdamhouse.com>.

| I have a reservation. | **Ik heb een reservering.** |
| What's the rate per night? | **Hoeveel kost het per nacht?** |

AIRPORT

Schiphol Airport (tel: 0900/0141 from inside Holland; tel: +3120 794 0800 from abroad; <www.schiphol.nl>), 14km (9 miles) from the city centre, is one of the busiest and most modern airports in Europe. It acts as a gateway to Europe for airlines from around the world. Its tax-free shopping centre is considered among the best in the world.

Every 10–30 minutes between 6am and 9pm a Connexxion Schiphol shuttle bus (tel: 038 339 4741; <www.schipholhotelshuttle.nl>) leaves the airport, making a stop at many of the major hotels in the city. Tickets (€12) are sold at the Connexxion counter in the arrivals hall and on the bus. The bus will also transport you back to the airport at the end of your stay (a return ticket cost €19).

There is a good rail connection from Schiphol Airport to Amsterdam Centraal Station (and onward to other cities in the Netherlands and to Brussels in Belgium). This Centraal Station connection runs 24 hours a day although there are fewer trains at night. The journey takes only 20 minutes.

B

BICYCLE HIRE *(fietsverhuur)*

Amsterdam is one of the most bicycle-friendly cities in the world, and cycling is a great way to get around it. You can hire bikes at MacBike at Mr Visserplein 2 near Waterlooplein, tel: 620 0985; <www.macbike.nl>, and at Stationsplein 12, tel: 624 8391; and at Rent-a-Bike Damstraat: Pieter Jacobsz Dwarsstraat 11, tel: 625 5029; <www.bikes.nl>. Try it for a day, or longer. If you want to take a tour by bicycle, Yellow Bike runs regular tours around the city or out into the countryside. Contact them at Nieuwezijds Kolk 29, tel: 620 6940; <www.yellowbike.nl>.

Remember that riding a bike in a busy city like Amsterdam is a potentially risky undertaking. Take extra care and watch out for trams, cars and other bicycles. It is advisable to wear a crash helmet, though most Amsterdammers don't. Also make sure that you are fully insured.

I'd like to hire a bicycle. **Ik zou graag een fiets huren.**

BUDGETING FOR YOUR TRIP

Airport transfer by bus: €12, by taxi €40, by train €3.60.

Accommodation: medium-quality double room for one night, €110–180.

Three-course dinner for one excluding drinks: €30–40.

Transport passes: day-pass €6.50, two-day pass €10.50, three-day €13.50 (valid on all forms of public transport).

Bicycle hire: €9 per day.

Car hire: compact car from €50 per day, medium-sized car €70.

Entrance to major museums: €10; under-19s go free.

Canal cruise: one-hour €9; **family dinner cruise:** around €70.

Flights to Amsterdam: from UK, schedule return flights average £125 plus tax; from New York, specials start at $350 plus tax.

C

CAMPING

There are a number of campsites within a few minutes' travel of the city centre. These are well run and open throughout the summer although they can fill up early, so it is sensible to make a reservation.

Camping Amsterdamse Bos is in the large park area to the south of the city with a direct bus link to Centraal Station; tel: 641 6868; fax: 640 2378; <www.campingamsterdamsebos.nl>. Vliegenbos Camping is located north across the IJ waterway in 25 hectares (60 acres) of woods; tel: 636 8855; fax: 632 2723; <www.vliegenbos.com>.

CAR HIRE

Amsterdam is a compact city with exceptionally good public transport and roads that favour bicycles. Parking is expensive and difficult to find in the city centre. Cars found along central canalsides and streets are wheel clamped automatically if they are parked illegally, or if the meter time has expired, and may be towed away.

If you are planning to stay in the city, it is unlikely to be worth considering vehicle rental; however, for touring the countryside it would certainly be worthwhile.

Most of the major international rental firms are represented in Amsterdam. You will also find agencies at Schiphol airport if you want to pick up a car directly from the airport.

Avis tel: 683 6061.

Budget tel: 612 6066.

Europcar tel: 683 2123.

Hertz tel: 201 3512.

Drivers must be over 21 (23 for some agencies, so check when making a reservation) and have held a full licence for at least 12 months. National or international licences must be shown at the time of renting. Collision damage waiver is available at extra cost but is well worth the peace of mind – but do check your own vehicle, household or cred-

| I'd like to hire a car today/tomorrow for one day/a week Please include full insurance. | Ik zou graag een auto willen huren vandaag/morgen voor één dag/één week Met een all-risk verzekering, alstublieft. |

it-card insurance before travelling, as you may already be covered. Prices start from around €50 per day for a compact car; a five-door hatchback (with more room) from €70 per day. Prices rise in peak season and drop if you hire the vehicle for more than a couple of days.

CLIMATE

The Netherlands has unpredictable weather patterns similar to those of Britain and is characterised by cold, wet winters and warm, wet summers. You can, however, have wonderful sunny days at any time of year, and Amsterdammers will always hope for long periods of bright, cold winter spells, which freeze the waterways for their favourite winter sport – ice skating. Unfortunately, this has not been happening very often in recent years.

Figures shown below are averages for each month and can vary.

	J	F	M	A	M	J	J	A	S	O	N	D
°C	7	8	11	13	16	18	20	21	17	14	11	8
°F	45	46	52	55	61	64	68	70	63	57	52	46

Rainfall is as follows (approximate conversions):

	J	F	M	A	M	J	J	A	S	O	N	D
mm	60	40	60	40	50	60	60	55	75	75	80	60
inch	2¾	1¾	2¾	1¾	2	2¾	2¾	2	3	3	3¼	2¾

CLOTHING

On a trip to Amsterdam, it's usually a good idea to take several different types of clothing, even if you are travelling in summer, when in theory it should be warm. A layering system is the best approach, so that you can take off or add clothing as you heat up or cool down. You should always take a rainproof outer layer, whenever you visit, and an umbrella. In winter, a thick coat or jacket will keep you warm in cold spells, when the wind can bite.

On warm summer days, shorts, T-shirts, light shirts and trousers or light dresses make ideal clothing. However, always carry an extra layer just in case, and take a light sweater or jacket for the evenings. Comfortable walking shoes are essential for the daytime, whatever time of year you travel.

Amsterdam is famous for being a casual city, but if you intend to eat at some of the finer restaurants, or visit the ballet or opera, a shirt and tie for men and 'dressy' ensemble for ladies is appropriate.

COMPLAINTS

In the first instance complaints should be taken up with the establishment concerned. If you are still dissatisfied then approach the VVV *(see page 129)* with complaints about hotels and restaurants and the Chamber of Commerce (tel: 531 4000) for other trade matters. They should be able to advise you further.

CRIME AND SAFETY *(see also EMERGENCIES and POLICE)*

Statistically, Amsterdam is one of the safest cities in Europe yet certain types of crime against visitors persist, notably luggage theft and pickpocketing. Always keep a watch on your luggage, especially when transferring it at the airport, Centraal Station, or to and from your hotel. Never carry cash, credit cards or passports in back pockets or an open handbag. Carry them close to your body, in a body belt or inside a pocket with a zip. Be especially watchful in the crowded squares and in the Red Light District.

As far as personal safety is concerned, after dark keep to well-lit major thoroughfares. You'll find that many Amsterdammers walk (or go by bicycle) to social engagements in town, so unless you are very late you will be walking on streets with other people. If in doubt, get a tram – they run until just before midnight, and there will probably be a stop near your hotel. Otherwise, take a taxi.

If you hire a car or take your own vehicle do not leave anything in the car, even in the glove compartment or boot – it would be wise to leave the glove box open to show thieves that there is nothing inside. If you do have anything stolen, report it immediately to the police.

A word on drugs: despite its relaxed attitude to (officially illegal, but tolerated) soft drugs (use of marijuana is allowed in a number of 'coffee shops'), the possession of hard drugs is still a criminal offence.

CUSTOMS AND ENTRY REQUIREMENTS

Citizens of the EU, US, Australia and New Zealand can visit for up to three months on production of a valid passport. South African citizens need a visa; contact the Netherlands Consulate General in Cape Town, tel: (021) 421 5660 for more details.

EU residents can import or export unlimited amounts of goods for personal use on which duty has been paid, although guidelines for personal use are as follows: 800 cigarettes, 400 cigars or cigarillos, 1kg tobacco, 10 litres of spirits, 90 litres of wine, 110 litres of beer.

Non-EU nationals or EU citizens travelling from non-EU countries can import tax-free goods to the following limits: 200 cigarettes or 50 cigars or 100 cigarillos, or 250g of tobacco, 1 litre of spirits or 2 litres of fortified or sparkling wine, 2 litres of wine, 50g of perfume, 0.25 litres of eau de toilette, 500g of coffee, 100g of tea.

If you are a non-EU resident (US, Canada, Australia, NZ, SA) you can receive a refund of up to 13.75 percent on the Value Added Tax paid on goods purchased in certain shops to take home. To qualify for a refund you must spend more than f50 in one shop in one day, and the goods must be exported out of the country within three months.

You must have the purchases, receipt and the refund cheque available for customs officials to view as you leave the country. For further information contact Tax-Free Shopping, tel: (023) 524 1909; fax: (023) 524 6164; <www.globalrefund.com>.

D

DRIVING

Vehicles are driven on the right in the Netherlands. At roundabouts, give way to traffic from the right (unless signs indicate otherwise).

Road conditions are generally good. Within Amsterdam itself the main thoroughfares are wide and in good condition. Canalside roads are narrow and generally open to traffic travelling in one direction (ie, up one side of the canal and down the other side). This adds to the difficulty of navigating. Just remember to keep the canal to your left and you can be sure that you are travelling on the correct side of the road.

(international) driving licence	**(internationaal) rijbewijs**
car registration papers	**kentekenbewijs**
green card (insurance)	**groene kaart**

Speed limits. In towns or built up areas: 30 or 50km/h (20 or 30mph). On dual carriageways and motorways: 120km/h (75mph) reduced to 100km/h (62.5mph) in wet weather. Other limits mays be posted.

Amsterdam has unique factors that drivers need to keep in mind. Always be aware of cyclists – they have their own traffic signals and cycle paths, but are still prone to ride without proper care and attention. Few cyclists use lights at night. Trams have priority over all other forms of transport, so watch out for them too; they also have their own signals on major roads. Be aware that tram tracks become very slippery when wet, so increase your stopping distances as necessary.

Many canalside roads have blind exits (they may be in dips, for instance). Both cyclists and car drivers can pull out without warning. Vehicles meeting on narrow canal bridges can cause problems. Road signs with arrows showing directional priority should be posted; if not, use good humour and common sense – and be prepared to reverse off the bridge to allow traffic to flow. Canalside roads and many other thoroughfares in the old part of the city can only accommodate one vehicle. This means that when delivery and rubbish lorries make their stops, vehicles behind them can be held up for many minutes.

If you travel to Amsterdam in your own car, you will need to carry your driving licence, registration document, or document of ownership, valid insurance, a red warning triangle in case of breakdown, and an international country identification sticker on the back of the car.

doorgaand verkeer	through traffic
eenrichtingsverkeer	one-way traffic
fietsers	cyclists
gevaarlijke bocht	dangerous bend
inhaalverbod	no overtaking (passing)
let op...	watch out for...
omleiding	diversion (detour)
parkeerverbod	no parking
pas op	attention
rechts houden	keep right
slecht wegdek	bad road surface
snelheid verminderen	reduce speed
uitrit	exit
verboden in te rijden	no entry for vehicles
verkeer over één rijbaan	single-lane traffic
voetgangers	pedestrians
wegomlegging	diversion
werk in uitvoering	roadworks in progress

Parking. Streetside and canalside parking is expensive and finding a parking space can take forever. Tickets are dispensed from machines found every 100m (100 yards) or so (you'll need change for the machines). Cars found without a parking ticket or found to be out of time will be clamped and a fine levied.

There are large car parks opposite Centraal Station (Parking Amsterdam Centre) and near Leidseplein (Europark); both open 24 hours a day. Parking costs from around €3.50 per hour or €45 per day. You can pay by credit card in these car parks.

Fuel. Petrol stations are plentiful both in the city and on main roads and motorways. Petrol is slightly cheaper than in the UK, but expensive by US and Canadian standards.

Fill it up, please, with…	**Vol, graag, met…**
super	**super**
regular	**normaal**
diesel	**diesel**

Assistance. If you need help the ANWB (Dutch Automobile Association; tel: 0800 000 888) offers roadside assistance. If you hire a car, make sure you get information about what to do if you break down.

I've broken down.	**Ik heb autopech.**
There's been an accident.	**Er is een ongeluk gebeurd.**

E

ELECTRICITY

The Netherlands operates on 230-volt/50-cycle current. Visitors from the UK or USA need an adapter for appliances. The better hotels may supply you with one, but they are easy to buy before you leave home. American 110-volt appliances require a transformer.

EMBASSIES AND CONSULATES

Although Amsterdam is the capital of the Netherlands, the diplomatic and political centre is Den Haag (The Hague) and all foreign embassies have their offices there.

Australia: Carnegielaan 4, 2517 KD Den Haag; tel: (070) 310 8200; <www.australian-embassy.nl>.

Canada: Sophialaan 7, 2514 JP Den Haag; tel: (070) 311 1600; <www.canada.nl>.

New Zealand: Carnegielaan 10, 2517 KH Den Haag; tel: (070) 346 9324; <www.nzembassy.com>.

Republic of Ireland: Doctor Kuijperstraat 9, 2514 BA Den Haag; tel: (070) 363 0993; <www.irishembassy.nl>.

South Africa: Wassenaarseweg 40, 2596 CJ Den Haag; tel: (070) 392 4501; <www.zuidafrika.nl>.

UK: Lange Voorhout 10, 2514 ED Den Haag; tel: (070) 427 0427; <www.britain.nl>.

US: Lange Voorhout 102, 2514 EJ Den Haag; tel: (070) 310 2209; <http://netherlands.usembassy.gov>.

Consulates in Amsterdam
UK: Koningslaan 44; tel: 676 4343; <www.britain.nl>.
US: Museumplein 19; tel: 575 5309; <http://netherlands.usembassy.gov>.

EMERGENCIES (see also POLICE)

For emergencies (fire, police or ambulance) dial **112**.

If you have a problem with theft or pickpocketing, there is a large police station at Lijnbaansgracht 219; tel: 0800 8844.

For non-urgent medical and urgent dental treatment, call **592 3434** (24 hours).

Call a doctor/ambulance.	**Bel een dokter/ziekenwagen.**
Call the police.	**Bel de politie.**
I have lost my passport.	**Ik ben mijn paspoort verloren.**
Help!	**Help!**

G

GAY AND LESBIAN TRAVELLERS

Amsterdam is an extremely friendly city for gay and lesbian visitors. There are hotels that cater specifically for gay and lesbian travellers and a vibrant social scene, with clubs that operate for gays or lesbians only.

There is a gay and lesbian community centre: COC, Rozenstraat 14; tel: 626 3087. The Gay and Lesbian Switchboard also has information about what's happening in the city (tel: 623 6565).

GETTING THERE

By air. Arrive at Amsterdam Airport Schiphol. Most of the world's major airlines operate flights to Schiphol, and KLM, the national airline of the Netherlands, has a large network and flies direct to the US, Canada and South Africa, and to Australia/New Zealand via Bangkok and Singapore.

It also has airline partners such as Air France in Europe and Northwest Airlines in the US. For reservations contact KLM at Schiphol on 474 7747, in the UK on 08705 074074, or toll-free in the USA on 800 225 2525. Other airlines that run nonstop services to Schiphol include Delta, Continental and United.

There are several flights to Schiphol daily from London airports, Manchester and other regional UK airports. Flights take around one hour. British Airways, BMI, easyJet and KLM all operate services.

By sea. There are several ferry services from Britain to the Netherlands. P&O Ferries operates a daily service from Hull to Rotterdam (tel: 08705 980333). There are also Stena Line sailings from Harwich to the Hook of Holland (tel: 08705 707070), and DFDS Seaways sailings from Newcastle to IJmuiden (tel: 08702 520524).

By rail. Travellers from Britain can use the Eurostar train service from London through the Channel Tunnel to Brussels, and onward from there by high-speed Thalys train. For those who wish to visit Amsterdam as part of a European rail tour, there are special prices for monthly passes and special ticket prices for under-26s and over-65s. Further details can be found on the website <www.euro rail.com>.

GUIDES AND TOURS

There are a number of qualified English-speaking guides who offer tours of the city. Some have specialities, some take groups or offer an individual service. Contact the VVV *(see page 129)* for a list.

A number of companies offer boat tours along the canals and these are probably the most popular activities in the city. Multilingual commentary keeps you informed about the attractions as you float along past them. Contact Rederij Lovers (tel: 622 2181; <www.lovers.nl>) or simply head to Damrak and Stationsplein and other docks from where the boats depart.

Yellow Bike offers accompanied bicycle tours of the city with English-speaking guides. Contact them on tel: 620 6940; <www.yellowbike.nl>.

H

HEALTH AND MEDICAL CARE

The Netherlands is a modern, well-run country, and its medical facilities are just the same. There are no health concerns about the city, although mosquitoes can be a nuisance in the summer, so anti-mosquito sprays or creams are useful. You will not need inoculations to travel here and the water is safe to drink.

Most doctors and other medical professionals speak English. Many proprietary brands of drugs are available over the counter from any pharmacy *(apotheek)*. A trained pharmacist will be able to give sound advice about medicines for minor ailments. Call 592 3434 to find out which pharmacies are open after hours and for referral to local doctors and dentists.

Always take out suitable travel insurance to cover any health problem you may have on your trip. You will be asked to pay for some medical treatment and should cover yourself against something serious happening to you. If you are an EU citizen, you will be covered for medical treatment if you have a European Health Insurance Card (EHIC). You will need to pay for treatment at the time but will be able to claim a refund on return.

HOLIDAYS

The following dates are official holidays:

1 January	*Nieuwjaar*	New Year's Day
30 April	*Koninginnedag*	Queen's Birthday
25–26 December	*Kerst*	Christmas

Moveable holidays are as follows:

Goede Vrijdag	Good Friday
Tweede Paasdag	Easter Monday
Hemelvaartsdag	Ascension Day
Tweede Pinksterdag	Whit Monday

All shops and offices are closed for all the above holidays.

INTERNET

The easyInternetcafé at Damrak 33 is open daily 9am–10pm. The Mad Processor at Kinkerstraat 11–13 (tel: 612 1818) is open daily from noon until 1 or 2am. The internet café Tops at Prinsengracht 480 is open noon–1am daily.

Each internet café has its own style and ambience, so choose accordingly. Some also have scanners, colour printers and other extras. Many hotels offer internet access.

L

LANGUAGE

There are around 30 million speakers of Dutch in the world, with Afrikaans (South Africa) and Flemish (Vlaams) of Belgium being closely allied to it. Its structure is similar to German, but it is grammatically simpler. That said, the Dutch usually speak English very well (and other languages passably), so you will rarely need to resort to your language phrasebook. However, knowing and using a few words of the language of the country you are visiting is only polite, and it may gain you some friendly comments.

Do you speak English?	**Spreekt u Engels?**
What does this mean?	**Wat betekent dit?**
I don't understand	**Ik begrijp het niet**
Good morning	**Goede morgen**
Good afternoon	**Goede middag**
Good evening	**Goeden avond**
Please/Thank you	**Alstublieft/Dank u**
You're welcome	**Alstublieft/Graag gedaan**

LAUNDRY AND DRY CLEANING

Most major hotels will organise laundry and dry-cleaning services for you at a price. If you wish to organise your own cleaning, there is a central laundry-cum-dry cleaners open seven days a week, 7am–9pm: Clean Brothers Wasserette at Kerkstraat 56; tel: 622 0273.

M

MAPS

The Tourist Office or VVV *(see page 128–9)* produces several different maps, which may be of use to travellers.

The Tourist Guide to Public Transport in Amsterdam has a map with public transport services superimposed on the basic city map. There is also the *City Map Amsterdam* – a simple map showing the location of all the major attractions.

For a very comprehensive map, Michelin's Amsterdam 1cm:150m map covers both the city centre and suburbs, with the city centre expanded for ease of use.

The *Insight Fleximap to Amsterdam* is detailed and easy to use, with a full street index and a laminated finish that means the frequent Amsterdam rain is not a problem.

MEDIA

Newspapers and magazines *(kranten, tijdschriften)*. Many English newspapers and magazines can be readily bought in the city. British daily papers are available soon after they are on sale at home. US papers will be a day old but the *International Herald Tribune* is published daily in Paris, so is on sale on the same day it is published. Most major hotels have a supply in their gift shops or at reception.

TV and radio *(televisie, radio)*. There are a number of Dutch television stations mainly serving the local community and sometimes taking services from various European countries (including British stations). The Dutch use subtitles to translate foreign programmes, rather than dubbing, so you will be able to understand the broadcasts – this is one of the reasons why the Dutch are so adept at speaking English and other languages. Most major hotels offer CNN and the BBC in your room.

In most places in the Netherlands you should be able to get a good reception for BBC radio transmissions.

MONEY MATTERS

In common with most other EU countries, the euro (€) is used in the Netherlands. Notes are denominated in 5, 10, 20, 50, 100, 200 and 500 euros; coins in 1 and 2 euros and 1, 2, 5, 10, 20 and 50 cents.

0	nul	10	tien	20	twintig
1	een	11	elf	21	eenentwintig
2	twee	12	twaalf	30	dertig
3	drie	13	dertien	40	veertig
4	vier	14	veertien	50	vijftig
5	vijf	15	vijftien	60	zestig
6	zes	16	zestien	70	zeventig
7	zeven	17	zeventien	80	tachtig
8	acht	18	achttien	90	negentig
9	negen	19	negentien	100	honderd

Currency can be exchanged in banks and bureaux de change offices that can be found at Centraal Station, in Leidseplein and in major shopping areas. Bureaux de change offices are open longer hours than banks. The GWK Travelex exchange office in Centraal Station provides a good service. Exchange rates and commission fees will be posted in the windows of these establishments. Travellers' cheques are accepted for commercial transactions and exchanged in the above establishments. You will need your passport to cash or use travellers' cheques. There's an American Express at Damrak 66, and a GWK Travelex office at Dam 23.

I'd like to change some pounds/dollars.	**Ik wil graag ponden/dollars wisselen.**
Do you accept travellers' cheques?	**Accepteert u reischeques?**

International ATMs are common and are indicated by the Cirrus or Plus signs on the machine. These machines also provide cash against MasterCard, Visa and other credit and charge cards.

Major credit cards are widely accepted in hotels, restaurants and shops, although there may be a minimum limit on payments in shops.

Can I pay with credit card?	**Kan ik met deze credit card betalen?**

O

OPENING TIMES *(see also HOLIDAYS)*

Offices and most government offices are generally open Mon–Fri 9am–5pm. Banks are open Mon–Fri 9am–4pm, extended to 5pm for main branches; late opening on Thur from 4.30pm–7pm.

The central post office at Singel 250 is open Mon–Fri 9am–6pm, Sat 10am–1.30pm. For VVV tourist offices *(see page 129)*.

Shops are generally open Mon 10am–6pm, Tues–Sat 9am–6pm, (9pm on Thur). Some shops open Sun noon–5pm. Many shops extend their opening hours in summer.

Monday	**maandag**	Friday	**vrijdag**
Tuesday	**dinsdag**	Saturday	**zaterdag**
Wednesday	**woensdag**	Sunday	**zondag**
Thursday	**donderdag**	tomorrow	**morgen**

P

POLICE *(see also EMERGENCIES)*

The police headquarters *(hoofdbureau van de politie)* is at Elandsgracht 117; tel: 0800 8844. There is also a large police station at

Lijbaansgracht 219; tel: 0800 8844. The emergency number is 112.
   Police stations can be found in the following central locations:
• Nieuwezijds Voorburgwal 104 (in the Red Light District)
• Nieuwmarkt (near Waag)
• Prinsengracht 1109.
   Police patrols are conducted in cars (see the word *politie* painted on the side) and on foot. Dutch police wear navy-blue uniforms and carry firearms as a matter of course. They are approachable to answer basic problems such as giving directions.

Can you help me?	**Kunt u mij helpen?**
Stop thief!	**Houd de dief!**

POST OFFICES

Post offices are distinguished by the TPG Post signs outside. They sell stamps, and change currency and travellers' cheques. The central post office is at Singel 250 and is open Mon–Fri 9am–6pm, Sat 10am–1.30pm. It is often busy, so avoid it if you only want to purchase stamps, which are available at the majority of shops selling postcards.

A stamp for this letter/
  postcard, please
	**Een postzegel voor deze brief/
	  briefkaart, alstublieft**

airmail	**luchtpost**
registered	**aangetekend**

PUBLIC TRANSPORT

Public transport in Amsterdam is excellent. The GVB municipal transport company runs a comprehensive system through the day, and a limited service through the night. You can use tickets or cards on buses, trams and metro (underground) services.

Pick up the *Tourist Guide to Public Transport in Amsterdam* leaflet at the VVV or GVB offices *(see page 129)*. If you intend to travel by bus after midnight, ask for the Nightbus leaflet, which details routes and running times.

OV-chipkaart. From 1 January 2009, if all goes according to plan, the only way to pay for public transport (trams, buses, the metro, and most rail services) in Amsterdam and throughout the Netherlands will be with a new travel card, the credit card-size OV-chipkaart – 'OV' stands for Openbaar Vervoer (public transport). The card is gradually being introduced on routes, during which time the old tickets and passes (see 'Strippenkaart' and 'Travel passes', below) will still be valid.

Three types of OV-chipkaart are available: personal, anonymous and throwaway. Although the personal card offers advantages to residents and long-stay visitors, short-term visitors will find the anonymous and throwaway cards simpler to acquire (although the throwaway card costs more per journey than the other two).

The personal and anonymous cards, both valid for five years, cost €7.50 and can be loaded and re-loaded with up to €30; the throwaway card costs €2.50. Electronic readers automatically deduct the correct fare as you travel. Reduced-rate cards are available for seniors and children. Note that, just like the old ticket system, the new cards are valid nationwide, so a card bought in Amsterdam can be used anywhere in the country.

Strippenkaart. The *strippenkaart* (strip card) is due to be phased out by the start of 2009, when the new OV-chipkaart takes over. It is a strip of small boxes (8, 15 or 45), one for each transport zone for each journey, plus you must count one extra box for the journey; so if you travel through two zones the *strippenkaart* should be stamped in the third box. (The central zone covers most major city attractions.) The card can be used by more than one person – just ensure you get a stamp for each person. Each stamp allows up to one hour's travel time. So you may transfer to another tram, metro or bus within the hour without getting another stamp. *Strippen-kaarten* are sold on trams and buses, by tobacconists and news-agents, and at VVV and GVB offices.

Travel passes. These provide one of the most affordable ways of travelling by public transport and are also are due to be phased out by the start of 2009, when the new OV-chipkaart takes over. Your pass allows you to travel on any form of public transport at any time for the duration of the pass. Day passes cost €6.50, but for more days it becomes even better value. A two-day pass costs €10.50, a three-day pass €13.50, and a four-day pass €16.50. Children's day passes cost €4.50.

But don't forget about the one-, two- or three-day I amsterdam Card *(see page 25)*, which allows substantial discounts on museum and free transport in the city. Tickets are available from VVV offices and at the GVB ticket office opposite Centraal Station.

Trams. Amsterdam's trams have some special safety issues: pressure on the bottom step at the entrance keeps the door open – important if you travel with elderly or very young passengers; many tram stops are in the middle of the road, with traffic passing on both sides – take care when getting on and off, and keep young children close to you; if a tram has a conductor you must enter at or towards the rear, otherwise enter by any door. Press one of the bells found at regular intervals along the carriage to get off at the next stop.

Museumboot. The Museum Boat runs along the canals between the major sights of the city. It runs at 45-minute intervals and is a fun way to travel. Day tickets cost €15 from the Rederij Lovers ticket office (tel: 530 1090; <www.lovers.nl>) opposite Centraal Station.

Water taxis. The Rederij Lovers company operates a number of water taxis so that you can personally tailor your trip. It is not for budget travellers, costing €30 for 15 minutes, but the boats can hold from eight to 44 people. Wine and cheese parties can be booked for romantic evenings, or you may just wish to book a journey back to your canalside hotel after an evening out. Contact Watertaxi at Stationsplein 8; tel: 535 6363; fax: 530 1090; <www.water-taxi.nl>.

Metro. The Amsterdam metro has four lines which are designed to link the city centre with the suburbs and as such are not as useful as other forms of public transport to the visitor touring attractions.

R

RELIGION

The Netherlands is a Christian country with various denominations of Protestant worshippers and Catholic communities. However, strict adherence to church worship has been declining steadily for many years and many churches, including several major churches in Amsterdam itself, have been deconsecrated. There is still a small population of Jews who hold synagogue services, and there is a significant Muslim minority. As the population has become more multinational, there are places of worship for several other religions.

Catholic Masses are held on Sundays at Sint-Nicolaaskerk (Prins Hendrikkade 73), Obrechtkerk (Jacob Obrechtstraat 28) and the Petrus en Pauluskerk (De Papegaai, Kalverstraat 58). The Anglican Church is at Groenburgwal 42. Jewish services are held at the Portugees-Israëlietische Synagoge, Mr Visserplein 3. The Jamai Mosque is at Reiner Claeszenstraat 4.

T

TELEPHONES

The international code for the Netherlands is 31, and the city code for Amsterdam is 020. To call a number within the city use just the seven-digit number. To call an Amsterdam number from other parts of the Netherlands, dial 020 first. If dialling from outside the country dial your international country code + 31 20 and the seven-digit number.

Most hotels have international direct dial (IDD) telephones but charge a high premium for long-distance and international calls. Calls using a credit or charge card may also cost more.

There are numerous public telephones around the city – most obviously outside Centraal Station and in the major squares – which take all major credit and charge cards.

Phone cards, available for €5, €10, €20 and €50, can be bought from newsagents and tobacconists.

To make an international call from Amsterdam, dial 00 and then the following country codes:

Australia **61**	South Africa **27**
Canada **1**	UK **44**
Ireland **353**	US **1**
New Zealand **64**	

TICKETS

You can obtain tickets for performances (theatre, opera, ballet, etc) from the VVV tourist offices *(see pages 128–9)* or the Amsterdam Uit Bureau (AUB). Contact them at Leidseplein or on tel: 0900 0191; <www.uitburo.nl>. If you have a credit card, they can book tickets for you and send them to your home address or arrange to have them waiting for you when you arrive in Amsterdam.

TIME DIFFERENCES

The Netherlands is one hour ahead of Greenwich Mean Time (GMT). From the last weekend in March to the last weekend in October, the clocks are advanced one hour – this change corresponds with the rest of the EU. During the European summer, the time differences are:

New York	London	**Amsterdam**	Jo'burg	Sydney	Auckland
6am	11am	**noon**	noon	8pm	10pm

TIPPING

Service charges are included in all bar, restaurant and hotel bills. However, an extra tip to show gratitude for good service is always appreciated. It is appropriate to leave the small change on the table in bars and cafés.

The following situations are still discretionary:

Taxi fares: round up the fare.

Hotel porter: €1–2 per bag.

Maid: €10 per week.

Lavatory attendant: €0.50 – although you may often have to pay this as an entry fee.

Tour guide: 10–15 percent.

Concierge: discretionary according to services provided.

TOILETS

There are few public toilet facilities in the city and the more or less open-to-view urinals – for men only – are pretty grim. However, department stores and the Magna Plaza mall have toilets, and many of the city's top hotels have toilets just off the lobby; there is often a €0.50 service charge for their use. Bars and cafés are designated public places, but it is considered polite to have a coffee or a beer if you use their facilities.

Where is the toilet?   **Waar is het toilet?**

TOURIST INFORMATION

For information before you depart, contact the Netherlands Board of Tourism and Conventions (NBTC) at the following addresses:

Head office: Nederlands Bureau voor Toerisme and Congressen, PO Box 458, 2260 MG Leidschendam, the Netherlands; tel: (+31 70) 370 5705; fax: (+31 70) 320 1654; <www.holland.com>.

Canada: 14 Glenmount Court, Whitby, Ontario, L1N 5M8; tel: (905) 666 5960; fax: (905) 666 5391;<www.holland.com>.

UK and Ireland: PO Box 30783, London WC2B 6DH; tel: (020) 7539 7950; premium-rate brochure line: 09068 717777; fax: (020) 7539 7953; e-mail: <info-uk@holland.com>; <www.holland.com>.

US: 355 Lexington Avenue, 19th Floor, NY 10017 New York; tel: (212) 370 7360; fax: (212) 370 9507; <information@holland.com>; <www.goholland.com>.

In Amsterdam

For information, maps, accommodation bookings and tickets while you are in Amsterdam, visit the VVV (Amsterdam Tourist Office) at the following addresses (note that they charge a small fee for many of their leaflets and maps):

• Stationsplein 10: opposite the entrance to Centraal Station, open daily 9am–5pm.

• Inside Centraal Station: at platform 2B, open Mon–Sat 8am–8pm, Sun and hols 9am–5pm.

• Leidseplein 1: at the intersection of Leidsestraat, open Sun–Thur 9.15am–5pm, Fri–Sat 9.15am–7pm.

Phone and fax numbers and website are the same for all the offices: tel: 551 2525; fax: 201 8850; e-mail: <info@atcb.nl>; <www.amsterdamtourist.nl>.

There is also a Holland Tourist Information bureau in Schiphol Airport, which is useful if you have not already booked your accommodation, and a GVB (public transport) information and ticket office at Stationsplein; tel: 0900 9292.

The magazine *Amsterdam Day by Day* lists events in the city.

tourist information office	**het bureau voor toerisme**
Do you have any information on...?	**Heeft u ook informatie over...?**
Are there any trips to...?	**Zijn er ook tochtjes naar...?**

W

WEBSITES

Many organisations such as museums and galleries have websites, and these have been included with telephone numbers in the appropriate sections; however, here are some websites that may help you to plan your trip:

• <www.amsterdamtourist.nl> is the VVV Amsterdam's own comprehensive website, with lots of travel information and news on the city's attractions.
• <www.noord-holland-tourist.nl> The North Holland tourist office website has information about Amsterdam and the surrounding areas.
• <www.visitholland.com> The Netherlands tourist office, with information about the whole country and standard tourist information.
• <www.amsterdamhotspots.nl> As its name suggests, this covers the hottest places for eating, drinking, dancing and much more.
• <www.dinner-in-amsterdam.nl> Useful for restaurant reviews.

WEIGHTS AND MEASURES

The metric system is used in the Netherlands.

Y

YOUTH HOSTELS

There are a number of youth hostels in the city. For more information about them, contact the Dutch youth hostel association, Stayokay, which is based at Professor Tulpstraat 2, 1018 HA Amsterdam; tel: 639 2929; <www.stayokay.com>.

Official Stayokay hostels offer discounts to members of the International Youth Hostel Association. The main one, Stayokay Amsterdam, with 540 beds, is at Vondelpark (Zandpad 5; tel: 589 8996; <www.stayokay.com/vondelpark>). Reservations are recommended at peak times.

Recommended Hotels

Many of Amsterdam's hotels are given a star rating by the Benelux Classification System, which rates hotels from five down to one star. The Netherlands Board of Tourism has rated more than 200 recommended hotels in the city, but there are also many unclassified boarding houses, which also represent good value.

Prices are high by international standards but quality is usually high too. In four- and five-star hotels all rooms have en-suite facilities; in three-star hotels generally all but a few rooms have their own facilities. The list below recommends hotels in locations around the city and in all classes. It features hotels with a particular character, location or facility that makes them stand out. They all accept major credit cards.

If you wish to make a phone or fax enquiry or book from abroad, dial 0031 20 before the seven-digit numbers given here.

The following price categories are for one night for two people in a double room with private facilities. Most large hotels charge 5 percent city tax in addition to room price; smaller hotels may include the tax in the price. Most hotels include breakfast in the price of the rooms, although some four- and five-star hotels charge for breakfast separately.

€€€€€	over 300 euros
€€€€	225–300 euros
€€€	150–225 euros
€€	75–150 euros
€	below 75 euros

THE CENTRE

Amstel Botel €€ *Oosterdokskade 2 4, 1011 AE Amsterdam; tel: 626 4247; fax: 639 1952; <www.amstelbotel.com>.* The only floating hotel in the city, this modern ship offers compact but tidy and modern rooms, all with TV and some with city views across the water. 176 cabins.

The Grand Amsterdam Sofitel Demeure €€€€€ *Oudezijds Voorburgwal 197, 1012 EX Amsterdam; tel: 555 3111; fax: 555*

3222; <www.thegrand.nl>. Built in 1578 as a Royal Inn, this building became Amsterdam City Hall following the loss of the Palace on the Dam and is situated in the heart of the old city. The exterior is an historic monument while the interior has been refurbished to an extremely high standard. There are excellent spa facilities at extra cost for guests. 182 rooms.

NH Barbizon Palace Hotel €€€€€ *Prins Hendrikkade 59–72, 1012 AD Amsterdam; tel: 556 4564; fax: 624 3353; <www.nh-hotels. com>*. A large five-star hotel, situated next to the Sint-Nicolaaskerk and opposite Centraal Station, which combines old canal houses with a modern entrance and reception area. All rooms have TV with CNN and Japanese channels, mini-bar, safe, trouser-press and modem plug. There's 24-hour room service as well as several restaurants, including the excellent Vermeer. Fitness room. 274 rooms.

Radisson SAS €€€€ *Rusland 17, 1012 CK Amsterdam; tel: 520 8300; fax: 520 8200; <www.radissonsas.com>*. Deep in the heart of Amsterdam, this stylish Scandinavian hotel incorporates old buildings that date as far back as the 17th century, and offers an eclectic range of design in its guest rooms. 242 rooms.

Rho Hotel €€ *Nes 5–23, 1012 KC Amsterdam; tel: 620 7371; fax: 620 7826; <www.rhohotel.com>*. A good-value hotel located on a quiet street one block back from Rokin. The building was once a theatre and retains several original features. Rooms are modern in style. 167 rooms.

THE SOUTHEAST

Canal House €€€ *Keizersgracht 148, 1015 CX Amsterdam; tel: 622 5182; fax: 624 1317; <www.canalhouse.nl>*. An intimate family-run hotel in a 17th-century canalside house. Each room is individually furnished and breakfast is taken in the old drawing room. Very friendly staff and a small bar. Breakfast included. 26 rooms.

Hotel De l'Europe €€€€€ *Nieuwe Doelenstraat 2–8, 1012 CP Amsterdam; tel: 531 1777; fax: 531 1778; <www.leurope.nl>*.

A member of the Leading Hotels of the World group, this centrally located hotel is housed in a building dating from 1896 but beautifully renovated to offer five-star luxury accommodation. The hotel has swimming pool, sauna/solarium and fitness centre. It also has 50 parking spaces. Breakfast is not included in the room price. 100 rooms.

InterContinental Amstel Amsterdam €€€€€ *Professor Tulpplein 1, 1018 GX, Amsterdam; tel: 622 6060; fax: 622 5808; <www.interconti.com>.* The 'grande dame' of Amsterdam hotels, situated directly on the River Amstel, has exquisite interiors; Internet access available. All rooms have a CD player, 30-channel TV and personal voicemail. The hotel has a health and fitness club with pool, sauna, gym and massage. 79 rooms.

Prinsenhof € *Prinsengracht 810, 1017 JL Amsterdam; tel: 623 1772; fax: 638 3368; <www.hotelprinsenhof.com>.* This hotel offers budget travellers a chance to experience life in an Amsterdam canal-house in a central location. The beamed rooms are bright, clean and thoughtfully furnished. Breakfasting with a view of the Prinsengracht is a boon. 10 rooms (six without bathroom).

Seven Bridges €€ *Reguliersgracht 31, 1017 LK Amsterdam; tel: 623 1329; fax: 624 7652; <www.sevenbridgeshotel.nl>.* Sitting on one of the prettiest canals, this B&B is among the most individual hotels in the city, with stylishly furnished rooms, stripped floorboards and antique furniture. There are no public rooms, so breakfast is served in your room. Note that access is via steep steps. No young children allowed. 11 rooms.

THE SOUTHWEST

Amsterdam American €€€€ *Leidsekade 97, 1017 PN Amsterdam; tel: 556 3000; fax: 556 3001; <www.amsterdamamerican. com>.* Situated amid the bars, restaurants and clubs of Leidseplein, the Art Deco American is the favoured hotel of celebrities and pop stars and is an historic monument. The rooms are double-glazed to eliminate the noise of the bars and cafés below. There is a gym and sauna. 174 rooms.

Golden Tulip Apollo Amsterdam €€€€ *Apollolaan 2, 1077 BA Amsterdam; tel: 673 5922; fax: 570 5744; <www.goldentulip. com>.* Situated in Amsterdam South, towards the RAI conference centre, this 5-star hotel is a good base for those who want to be a little way from the hubbub of the city. Situated in a wide canal basin, the hotel has wide waterside terraces and a marina. Rooms have mini-bar, trouser-press and TV with in-house video. 219 rooms.

Hotel Acro €€ *Jan Luijkenstraat 44, 1071 CR Amsterdam; tel: 662 5538; fax: 675 0811; <www.acro-hotel.nl>.* Situated in a quiet street surrounded by private residences, in the vicinity of Museumplein and a few minutes' walk from Vondelpark and Leidseplein, the Acro is a modern, functional hotel. 65 rooms.

Hotel De Filosoof €€ *Anna van den Vondelstraat 6, 1045 GZ Amsterdam; tel: 683 3013; fax: 685 3750; <www.hotelfilosoof.nl>.* Situated on the north side of Vondelpark, a little way out of town, this unique hotel is run by a philosophy teacher, who attracts many like-minded guests. Rooms are named after famous philosophers and are individually designed. Bar/lounge and library and attractive garden, but no restaurant. 38 rooms.

Hotel Nicolaas Witsen €€ *Nicolaas Witsenstraat 48, 1017 ZH Amsterdam; tel: 623 6143; fax: 620 5113; <www.hotelnicolaas witsen.nl>.* Situated on a side street around 15 minutes' walk from the city centre and five minutes south of Museumplein. All rooms have TV. This is a good hotel for its classification, with ample breakfasts. 29 rooms.

Museum Hotel €€€ *P.C. Hooftstraat 2, 1071 BX Amsterdam; tel: 662 1402; fax: 673 3918; <www.hotel-museum.com>.* Situated near Museumplein and Leidseplein. This is a value option for independent travellers and is also popular with tour groups. The airport shuttle stops in front of the hotel. 110 rooms.

Museum Square Hotel Amsterdam €€€ *De Lairessestraat 7, 1071 NR; tel: 671 9596; fax: 671 1756; <www.museumsquare hotel.nl>*. A small hotel opposite the Concertgebouw, a couple of minutes from Museumplein. The rooms are modern and clean, with mini-bar, hair-dryer and TV. 34 rooms.

Park Hotel €€€€ *Stadhouderskade 25, 1071 ZD Amsterdam; tel: 671 1222; fax: 664 9455; <www.parkhotel.nl>*. Across the street from Leidseplein and only minutes from Museumplein, the Park Hotel has a bar and a restaurant serving Dutch cuisine. 187 rooms.

Toro Hotel €€€ *Koningslaan 64, 1075 AG Amsterdam; tel: 673 7223; fax: 675 0031; <www.hoteltoro.nl>*. Two Edwardian houses set in ample gardens now converted into a stylish hotel. Situated on the south side of Vondelpark. All rooms have TV, safe and mini-bar. The hotel also has a car park. 22 rooms.

THE NORTHWEST

The Ambassade €€€ *Herengracht 341, 1016 AZ Amsterdam; tel: 555 0222; fax: 555 0277; <www.ambassade-hotel.nl>*. Ten historic canal houses have been amalgamated to create The Ambassade, situated within a few minutes' walk of the city centre. The rooms are nicely furnished, and the hotel offers 24-hour room service, although it has no restaurant. All rooms have a trouser-press, mini-bar and safe, and there is a lift to the upper floors. 59 rooms.

Die Port van Cleve €€€ *Nieuwezijds Voorburgwal 176–180, 1012 SJ Amsterdam; tel: 622 6429; fax: 622 0240; <www.dieport vancleve.com>*. Situated just behind the Royal Palace, the hotel has an ornate façade and a historic bar with Delft tile decoration. In addition to rooms it also has suites that can accommodate up to eight people. 120 rooms.

Hotel Belga € *Hartenstraat 8, 1016 CB Amsterdam; tel: 624 9080; fax: 623 6862; <www.hotelbelga.nl>*. Situated in the heart of the old town, the Belga is a good budget option for those who want to be in the centre of Amsterdam. Not all rooms have en-suite facilities, so do specify when you make your booking. All rooms have cable TV and telephones. 10 rooms.

NH Grand Hotel Krasnapolsky €€€€ *Dam 9, 1012 JS Amsterdam; tel: 554 9111; fax: 622 8607; <www.nh-hotels.com>*. This large imposing hotel sits opposite the Royal Palace on the Dam, in the very heart of the old town. Rooms have safe, hairdryer, minibar and TV; the hotel has several restaurants. There is also a pretty interior garden with terrace. Parking facilities. 469 rooms.

Tulip Inn Dam Square €€€ *Gravenstraat 12–16, 1012 NM Amsterdam; tel: 623 3716; fax: 638 1156; <www.tulipinndam square.com>*. Housed in the building of an old distillery, this cosy hotel has a thoroughly modern interior. Pleasant, quiet and friendly, it is only minutes from the centre. 38 rooms.

AT SCHIPHOL AIRPORT

There are many hotels around Schiphol International Airport, which is 20 minutes by train from the city centre. Most belong to large international groups but you may need to stay near the airport.

Dorint Novotel Amsterdam Airport €€€€ *Sloterweg 299, 1171 VB Badhoevedorp; tel: 658 8111; fax: 658 8100; <www.dorint.de>*. This hotel, five minutes from the airport, has a free shuttle to the terminal and daily transport to the Rijksmuseum. It also has good connections with motorways and has ample parking. The hotel features a restaurant and sauna/solarium, and has squash and tennis courts affiliated to it. 222 rooms.

Sheraton Amsterdam Airport Hotel €€€€€ *Schiphol Boulevard 101, 1118 BG Schiphol; tel: 316 4300; fax: 316 4399; <www.sheraton.com/amsterdamair>*. This five-star hotel is directly linked to the airport terminal, offering convenient transfer from room to railway station for access to the city. The hotel has an indoor pool, sauna and fitness centre. Air-conditioned, soundproofed rooms with data ports. 24-hour room service and several restaurants. 406 rooms.

Recommended Restaurants

Amsterdam offers an extensive choice of cuisine. Standards are high, and prices are reasonable for a major city, although there are relatively few budget options. You'll find many small restaurants by simply strolling along the canalside streets and narrow alleyways of the city centre. Since lunch tends to be a snack for the Dutch, most restaurants don't open until the evening.

Amsterdam specialises in small, intimate eateries. Most would prefer you to make a reservation but many restaurants accommodate customers who arrive on spec. Few restaurants have dress codes, but at the higher-class establishments it would be advisable to ask first, just in case.

This list of recommended restaurants concentrates on interesting, independent establishments, although a couple of outstanding hotel restaurants are also included. The following price categories are for a three-course dinner per person without drinks. Wine can be expensive, although many restaurants stock house wine at reasonable cost. Our listed restaurants accept all major international credit cards, unless otherwise noted.

€€€€€	over 60 euros
€€€€	45–60 euros
€€€	30–45 euros
€€	20–30 euros
€	below 20 euros

THE CENTRE

Hemelse Modder € *Oude Waal 11; tel: 624 3203*. A mixture of vegetarian and meat dishes with French and Italian influences. All ingredients used are deliciously fresh. Daily specials. Open Tues–Sun 6pm–12.30am.

In de Waag €€ *Nieuwmarkt 4; tel: 422 7772*. The atmospheric setting of this bar/restaurant, in the Gothic splendour of the old Weigh House with its huge beams, would be enough to recommend it. The décor echoes this structure with huge tables for feasting. A mixed menu of fusion-style dishes. Open daily 10am–midnight.

Pier 10 €€€ *De Ruyterkade, Steiger (Pier) 10; tel: 624 8276.* Back in business after being deconstructed during rebuilding work on the harbour installations behind Centraal Station, this small waterfront gem in a former shipping company office serves fine seafood and Continental cuisine, complemented by views of the bustling IJ waterway. Open daily noon–3pm and 6.30pm–1am.

Restaurant Vermeer €€€€ *(in the NH Barbizon Palace Hotel) Prins Henrikkade 59–72; tel: 556 4885.* One of the finest restaurants in Amsterdam, serving a French menu with Dutch and Continental influences. Open Mon–Fri noon–2.30pm and 6–10pm, Sat 6–10pm.

Wilhelmina-Dok €€€ *Nordwal 1; tel 632 3701.* This waterfront restaurant adds a touch of adventure to unfashionable Amsterdam North. You need to take a short, free ferry trip from Centraal Station to partake of its wide-ranging continental menu. A fabulous, if often windswept, enclosed terrace affords a perfect viewpoint for observing the maritime comings and goings on the IJ waterway. Open daily 11am–midnight.

THE SOUTHEAST

D'Vijff Vlieghen €€€€ *Spuistraat 294–302; tel: 530 4060.* The rather uninviting name of 'The Five Flies' should not put you off. Old Dutch décor, New Dutch cuisine with a good range of *jenevers*. Open daily 6–11pm.

Dynasty €€€ *Reguliersdwarsstraat 30; tel: 626 8400.* This place offers a tempting choice of Thai, Vietnamese and Chinese dishes all conveniently under one roof. You can choose from the set menus or go à la carte to mix and match your meal from different countries. The food is beautifully prepared from fresh ingredients. The colourful dining room has a ceiling covered in parasols. Open Wed–Mon 5.30–11pm.

Haesje Claes €€ *Spuistraat 273–275; tel: 624 9998.* Comfortable, old-fashioned restaurant full of nooks and crannies decorated with Delftware and hanging lamps. Wide-ranging menu but traditional Dutch dishes (especially stews) and steaks are best value. Open daily noon–10pm.

Het Tuynhuys €€€ *Reguliersdwarsstraat 28; tel: 627 6603.* Mediterranean cuisine and bistro-style décor, in a former coach-house with a beautiful courtyard where you can eat out in summer. Open Mon–Fri noon–2.30pm and 6–10.30pm, Sat–Sun 6–10.30pm.

Kantjil de Tijger €€ *Spuistraat 291–293; tel: 620 0994.* Some of the most authentic Indonesian food served in a modern but soothing Art Deco-influenced dining room. There are vegetarian dishes on the menu. Open Mon–Fri 4.30–11pm, Sat–Sun noon–11pm.

La Rive €€€€€ *(in the InterContinental Amstel Amsterdam Hotel) Professor Tulpplein 1; tel: 520 3264.* This formal French restaurant offers a gastronomy extravaganza and its food is exceptional (it's the only establishment in the city to have earned two Michelin stars). Excellent wine list. Pretty riverside setting. Reservations recommended. Open Mon–Fri noon–2pm and 6.30–10.30pm, Sat 6.30–10.30pm.

Rose's Cantina €€ *Reguliersdwarsstraat 38–40; tel: 625 9797.* Busy Mexican restaurant serving large portions of Tex-Mex cuisine, including *enchiladas*, *tortillas*, *fajitas* and sizzling *chimichangas* plus a range of burgers. Pitchers of margarita also available. Open Mon–Sat 5.30–11 30pm, Sun 3–11.30pm.

Sluizer €€€ *Utrechtsestraat 41–45; tel: 622 6376.* The plain wooden tables and simple elegant decoration in Sluizer could grace any French bistro. You'll find two restaurants in one here with a choice of excellent seafood – mussels a speciality – or French cuisine. Open daily 5–11pm.

The Tara Irish Pub € *Rokin 85–89; tel: 421 2654*. An authentic pub atmosphere with pub food such as beef and ale pies and hotpots. Good, hearty and filling. Open daily 11am–11pm, later at weekends.

Tempo Doeloe €€ *Utrechtsestraat 75; tel: 625 6718*. For years one of the best performers on the city's Indonesian cuisine circuit. Its elegant décor adds a touch of class to the experience. A too-literal interpretation of the word *pedis* (hot) might bring tears to your eyes, but only a few dishes are so spicy that they must be handled with care. Reservations essential. Open daily 6–11.30pm.

Visrestaurant Lucius €€€ *Spuistraat 247; tel: 624 1831*. Lucius specialises in seafood and fish dishes, ranging from huge plates of mussels to salmon to oysters. There is a range of more exotic species such as swordfish, and a more limited choice for meat eaters. Open daily 5pm–midnight.

THE SOUTHWEST

Le Garage €€€ *Ruysdaelstraat 54–56; tel: 679 7176*. This exciting bar/brasserie is owned and operated by Joop Braakhelike who presents his own cooking programme on Dutch TV. The atmosphere is bright and breezy and the food is influenced by the cuisine of France. Open lunch Mon–Fri noon–2pm and 6–11pm, Sat–Sun 6–11pm.

Pygma-Lion €€ *Nieuwe Spiegelstraat 5a; tel: 420 7022*. This funky South African bistro serves exotic meats such as ostrich, although there are also more mainstream choices, along with salads and sandwiches. Open Tues–Sun 5.30–11pm.

Vertigo €€ *Vondelpark 3; tel: 612 3021*. The Film Museum's café-restaurant is a star in its own right, with a cosy basement café and a prime location looking out on leafy Vondelpark for its outdoors terrace – there's no better place in town to sample Mediterranean-inspired fusion cuisine on a languid summer evening. Open daily 10am–1am.

THE NORTHWEST

Akitsu Japanese Restaurant €€€ *Rozengracht 228–230; tel: 625 3254*. In the Jordaan, serving a range of hot entrées along with some sushi and sashimi. Open Tues–Sun 6–10pm.

Bolhoed €€ *Prinsengracht 60–62; tel: 626 1803*. The 'Bowler Hat' is housed in a former milliner's shop with a tiny waterside terrace and brings zest to vegetarian dining. Open daily noon–11pm.

Christophe' €€€€ *Leliegracht 46; tel: 625 0807*. Despite the departure of its eponymous founder, celebrated chef Jean-Christophe Royer, this canalside restaurant has continued under new ownership in his tradition of creating fine French cuisine with a modern touch and superior wines. Open Tues–Sat, 6.30–10.30pm.

De Silveren Spiegel €€€€ *Kattengat 4–6; tel: 624 6589*. You won't find a more typically Old Dutch-looking place than this. The menu is an updated interpretation of Dutch cuisine, with French added for respectability. Open daily 5.30–10.30pm.

De Vliegende Schotel € *Nieuwe Leliestraat 162–168; tel: 020 625 2041*. The 'Flying Saucer' doesn't quite live up to the speedy implication in its name, but this Jordaan eatery lands some out-of-this-world vegetarian and vegan cuisine. Open daily 4–11.30pm.

Manzano €€€ *Rozengracht 106; tel: 624 5752*. Spanish restaurant with a relaxed bistro-style atmosphere. Serves everything from tapas to authentic paella. Open Sun–Thur 5–10.30pm, Fri–Sat 5–11pm.

Pancake Bakery € *Prinsengracht 191; tel: 625 1333*. Choose from around 70 different oversized Dutch pancakes, savoury or sweet, in this atmospheric warehouse. Open daily noon 9.30pm.

Treasure €€ *Nieuwezijds Voorburgwal 115–117; tel: 623 4061*. This popular place serves what is probably the most authentic Chinese cuisine in the city, with several regional styles on the menu. Dim-sum bar. Open daily noon–11pm.

INDEX

Berlitz pocket guide

Amsterdam

Tenth Edition 2008

Written by Lindsey Bennett
Updated by George McDonald
Edited by Clare Peel
Series Editor: Tony Halliday

No part of this book may be reproduced,
stored in a retrieval system or transmitted
in any form or means electronic,
mechanical, photocopying, recording or
otherwise, without prior written permission
from Berlitz Publishing. Brief text
quotations with use of photographs are
exempted for book review purposes only.

All Rights Reserved
© 2008 Berlitz Publishing/Apa
Publications GmbH & Co. Verlag KG,
Singapore Branch, Singapore

Printed in Singapore by Insight Print
Services (Pte) Ltd, 38 Joo Koon Road,
Singapore 628990. Tel: (65) 6865-1600.
Fax: (65) 6861-6438

Berlitz Trademark Reg. U.S. Patent Office
and other countries. Marca Registrada

Photography
Glyn Genin/Apa 6, 9, 12, 26, 32, 33, 37, 43, 44,
45, 46, 50, 56, 65, 68, 69, 83, 84, 86, 91, 92, 95,
99; Guglielmo Galvin/Apa 1, 8, 22, 29, 49, 54,
61, 64, 66, 67, 71, 75, 76, 79, 80, 85, 88, 102,
103; Pete Bennett/Apa 19, 20, 28, 34, 38, 40,
42, 51, 53, 55, 63, 73, 77, 97, 98; Bill Wassman/
Apa 10, 14, 24, 96; Amsterdam Historical
Museum 16; David Beatty/Apa 87; Jon
Davison/Apa 30; Tom Le Bas/Apa 101; Dirk-
Jan Visser/World Picture Network 58/9.

Cover picture: Jean-Pierre Lescourret/
Jupiter Images

Every effort has been made to provide
accurate information in this publication,
but changes are inevitable. The publisher
cannot be responsible for any resulting
loss, inconvenience or injury.

Contact us

At Berlitz we strive to keep our guides as
accurate and up to date as possible, but if you
find anything that has changed, or if you have
any suggestions on ways to improve this guide,
then we would be delighted to hear from you.

Berlitz Publishing, PO Box 7910,
London SE1 1WE, England.
fax: (44) 20 7403 0290
email: berlitz@apaguide.co.uk
www.berlitzpublishing.com